Come Back Kinda Love

ERIKA DANIELS

EXPLORA BOOKS
700 – 838 West Hastings St. Vancouver, BC V6C 0A6
www.explorabooks.com
Phone: (604) 330 6795

ISBN: 978-1-998394-68-5 (Paperback)
978-1-998394-72-2 (Hardback)
978-1-998394-71-5 (eBook)

Come Back Kinda Love

A NOVEL BY ERIKA DANIELS

For My Daughter.

Introduction

I wrote this book over a few weeks in the fall of 2012, shortly after I published my first book, "On the Rocks, Marriage and Margaritas." My grief and pain was still very raw then. I spent months editing it, almost a year, and then deleted it from my laptop in 2013 because it was so deeply personal and emotional for me. It stayed that way until earlier this year when I started thinking about the book again, whether I could handle the contents and raw feeling that comes with divorce and loving again. My publishing company helped me find software tools that could recover the deleted files, unprotect the password and get me back on my way to publishing it, now over 10 year later.

I have found over the years that my story is so common, too common, yet nobody talks or writes about the agony of divorce and moving on after infidelity. I wrote this book with love in my heart for others recovering from such an awful life experience. I wrote this book for my kids, to help them understand that the heartbreak was real and painful. I have no regrets on how I have lived my life. There is no timeline on grief and no expiration date for finding a 'Come Back Kinda Love.'

CHAPTER ONE

It's a warm, autumn Saturday in late September, with falling leaves everywhere, a picturesque day for a wedding. There is a high sun and a soft breeze to cool down the 85-degree temperature in the air. In the lines of trees across the valleys where I live, the colors are vivid. Today there are reds and oranges, golds and browns. A few greens are scattered in the landscape too, holding out a little longer, trying to avoid the inevitable that comes with colder weather. The world looks like a microbrewery of sorts, ambers, ales, nut browns.

There is a farmer in a tractor off in the distance picking beans in the field about a half mile from my house, as the crow flies. The churning of the engine seems to be urging me to get outside and enjoy the day. I've been watching from my bedroom window, begging for mercy from a headache that won't quit. I've been laying in the wrought-iron bed that I was accused of "stealing" out of the guest suite from the home that I shared with my family before it was pried apart by infidelity. In fact, in his humble opinion, I took "everything." He got the 5,000 square foot house on 40 acres in the country, with the in-ground pool and 11,000 newly planted trees surrounding it. He got the damn dogs. I suspect he'll even get my best friend out of the deal. Me, I got the bedroom set that I bought online for 700 bucks, a couple of 10-year-old hunter green leather couches, a few occasional tables, a dining room set that doesn't even fit my space, and a camouflage ATV with a bucket on the back. I figure I'll use that bucket to store all the bullshit he is going to shovel at me and my kids the next few years, trying to lie his way out of the bad choices he's made.

I've been trying to convince myself that I'm going to be better off. So now, being here in this place in my life, a 35-year-old, soon-to-be-single, mother of three, I plan on celebrating with a little bit of fun and a drink in my hand. And I've been celebrating just about every damn day. I don't even really know what else to do with myself. Last night was a very drunk, very late night out in my hometown of 3,000-something, a four in the morning kind of party. It's one of many in the last few weeks, exploring my newfound freedom after the coward announced that he wanted a divorce on the last day of July.

A week ago, my cousin Alicia sent me a text, asking if I wanted to go along to the wedding of a young couple from town.

Hey, you have your kids next Saturday?

No, why

Alicia knows that my kids are the center of my world, and she already knows I won't do anything else but be with them if it's my weekend to have them. My kids have already been through so much, the lies, the cheating, watching me slowly fall apart with the realization that I could not save my marriage.

My 13-year-old, Bryce, is taking it the hardest. His coming of age interrupted by the selfishness of his dad's penis. His 9-year-old brother, Bennett, doesn't really understand the messiness of the whole thing. Our 6-year-old daughter, Becca, who I pray will never have to endure the infidelity of her own husband, does not remember me ever living in the house that our family shared. On the day we told the kids that we were going to separate, Bennett got up from the living room couch and quietly left the room while his older brother sobbed, and his little sister watched him. They are all just beginning to realize that whatever family life they do remember, however chaotic or dysfunctional it might have been at times, is never going to be the same again.

The suspense is making my stomach hurt. Finally, she shoots me a text back.

> Wedding for Ben and Deanne
>
> I RSVP'd for Nick but he doesn't want to go anymore
>
> > Well, is it ok with Deanne?
>
> I don't know, why
>
> > Well, I don't want to just show up with you
>
> It's fine, trust me
>
> > No, I'm not going to just show up
>
> Seriously, she isn't going to care
>
> > Just ask her
>
> OK, I'll get back to you

Alicia is 11 years my junior and the godmother of my baby girl. I babysat Alicia and her baby brother when they were young. I remember when she was born. I remember when her brother came along and rocked the sweet little world that surrounded her after being alone with her parents for the first 7 years of her life. Alicia called me 'GG' because she couldn't say my real name. At 12, her dad adorned me with the nickname 'Thumper,' when my size 10 feet were quickly catching my age. Her family lived down the street from us, in a neighborhood shaped like a shamrock, with three cul-de-sacs centered by my best friend's cozy white split-level situated on a double lot where we placed an ice cream bucket for our neighborhood games of Kick the Can. As we got older, our families played Chase the Ace and Pictionary on Friday nights, while our parents drank beer. Through the neighbor's yards, I could race home and back in 3 minutes to get whatever my mom had forgotten to bring, or just get more beer. Alicia would be patiently waiting for me at the door when I returned.

Right now, she is exactly the person I need to help me pull through the biggest heart break of my life. Maybe she can be my babysitter for a little while. God knows I'm going to need it. She reminds me of who I am, of my childhood. I feel like she will keep me sane, grounded, if there is even the slightest possibility of that. Last summer, she let me stay at her house when I didn't have my kids and I needed a place to crash. I hung out with her and her group of friends, a bunch of young women with independent spirits and hearts like mine. She listened to my ranting and raving. She helped me move into my new house. She tolerated my partying.

A few minutes later, I get a text back from her.

> Hey, I talked to Deanne

> > What'd she say?

> She said you're more than welcome to come

> > OK, well, let me think about it

I don't even really know the bride and groom very well. We talked about their wedding while we played a couple of games of bingo at the local American Legion a few nights last summer, but that's about it. Not that I wouldn't still dance with the bride to the whole, "I Knew the Bride When She Used to Rock and Roll" gig, but I don't want to be a wedding crasher either. I think about it a moment longer.

> Hell, why not

It's my first wedding as a single woman. Hopefully there will be free beer. I'm going to have witness "wedding bliss" sooner or later anyway. It might as well be now. It might as well be with her. I hope that drinks will love me through it.

About 1:30, I get cold feet, and it's not even my wedding day. I don't want to be a flake, but my freaking head hurts so badly I can hardly breathe. It's one of those moments that I have to either shit or get off the pot, lay in my comfortable bed or escape to the brisk air of the shower. I send a text to Alicia to find out how mad she'll be if I don't go along with her.

> > So how's it going?

> > > Good, heading to the bar in a little while

> > How mad are you going to be if I don't go?

> > > Why, why wouldn't you go?

My freaking head hurts

Well you shouldn't have stayed out so late last night

Yeah, tell me something I don't know

It's up to you

I know it is, but I don't want you to be mad at me either

I want you to go, I don't want to go alone

I pause another moment before responding, looking back over the conversation. The coziness of my bed is just so perfect right now, bright sunshine spilling on my face like the hot water of the shower that I should be taking. It reminds me of when I was growing up, when I would lay on the floor of the living room in the house that my parents built and lived in for almost 30 years. The room faced west so I sprawled out on the warm, plush carpet like a cat, soaking up the late afternoon sun as it spilled over my body. I remember how my mom would be making dinner in the neighboring kitchen, aromas of hot dishes and homemade bread passing through to where I would lay on the floor. Alicia's text interrupts my daydreaming.

So what are you gonna do

I don't know, I just feel like hell right now

Well get up and get in the shower and you'll feel better

I know, you're right

I swing my legs over the side of the bed and my phone vibrates again.

Are you up

Not yet

Well, get going

Ok, I'm going

You better be

I am, see you in an hour

CHAPTER TWO

The wedding ceremony is at 3, but we're skipping it. I am thankful that Alicia is not subjecting me to that kind of torture just weeks after I spent three hours in painful mediation, trying to untangle what almost 13 years of marriage brought together. Attending a wedding ceremony today would only remind me of my own wedding so many years ago in late October. The ominous clouds and sturdy wind blowing and spitting a light rain all day long, almost predicting the kind of outcome that was inevitable for us.

I was so young then, much younger than the couple about to be married today. Having already had my oldest son six months before, I felt older than 22, a little more mature than the high school and college friends who came from such a distance to see their first friend tie the knot. I suppose the wedding was the talk of the town, maybe because the groom was such a Casanova, but probably because a good Catholic girl like me had been baptized into motherhood a little too soon.

Alicia and I are going to meet at The Saloon to have some drinks before we head to the reception. I love the outfit I am wearing. I devoted two lunch hours shopping at the mall earlier in the week looking for the perfect dress for the day. It's a sheath-style with black, cream and brown swipes across it, highlighted by my brown hair with auburn kisses from the summer I spent on the golf course commiserating the death of my marriage. The upper bodice occasionally opens to display some cleavage and the skirt wraps around but shows some thigh every now and then. I feel like a different woman now, more confident, self-assured, like people don't even recognize me. Of course, it always helps to shed 35 pounds in 3 months with the onslaught of divorce and during the process, discover that your ex was banging your best friend.

When I walk in, everyone turns and stares. It feels like a moment out of the old 80s sitcom, Cheers, where folks turn and gawk when anyone enters the establishment. There is a huge wrap-around, 30-foot bar straight ahead, six or seven TVs hanging from the ceilings around the bar, some low tables directly to the right of the front door, and a few high-tops against a wall on the way back to the kitchen. Beyond the low tables, the dance-floor-by-night shares space with a pool table, which is mostly unused except for Thursday league nights.

I wave at Alicia, who is sitting on the other side of the bar by the high-tops with a few of her friends who went to the wedding. There are two guys sitting at the corner of the bar closest to the door. I stand beside the open chair that is next to them, waiting for the bartender to serve me. They are staring at me, so I turn to them and smile.

"Is this seat open, gentlemen?" I ask.

The guy seated closest to the chair motions toward it.

"For you, it is," he says.

"Well, thank you, sir," I say, as I slide into the seat and order a beer.

He's the dad of one of my youngest son's friends.

"Looking good, woman," he says with a smile.

"Hey, thanks," I tell him.

The guy sitting next to him leans forward and looks over at me.

"Yeah, you clean up pretty good," he says, like I'm some tomboy who has never worn a dress before.

"Where you headed tonight?" he asks.

"I'm going as Alicia's date to Ben and Deanne's wedding, down at Snowball's," I say. "It's my first wedding as a single woman, so it should be interesting."

"Yikes, well it could be dangerous with you lookin' like that," he says, laughing as he tips his beer back to finish it. "We're heading to the casino for a couple of hours, but maybe we'll stop there on our way back home."

"OK, well, maybe see you later on then," I tell them.

He motions to the bartender to come over so they can pay their tab. They both stand up to go, leaving me sitting there alone. A few minutes later, Alicia comes over from the other side of the bar.

"Hey there," I say, as she drops her tiny frame down into the chair next to me.

She's wearing a black sateen sheath dress that enhances her natural double Ds, pushing them up over the bandeau top.

"Hey," she says, flashing me her killer white smile and rare bluish-green eyes. "Lookin' good, lady."

"Well, thanks, you too. Love that dress," I tell her. "Where'd you get it?"

"Oh, I've had it a while, but I think it's Express," she says, looking down at herself and straightening the skirt.

"I feel like hell," I admit. "Are you hungover today?"

"I was this morning, but now I feel good," she says. "But I started drinking a couple of hours ago."

She's young and wild and free. Apparently, she tolerates this party girl lifestyle a little better than me. Around 5, we leave the bar to head to the reception. On the way down in the car that she has affectionately named "Jerry," we chat about my night out and her friends' observations of the events at the church. She moves on to rambling about her boyfriend as I admire the fall day. The colors in the trees pop out of the countryside, like a panoramic Ansel Adams picture celebrating the beauty of the season.

Snowball's Bar and Grill is in the middle of nowhere really, in the middle of the boondocks, which usually makes it just the right location for an excuse to have a hell of a good time. It is nicely nestled at the intersection of two county roads. The one that we drove down was a gravel mess for many, many years, but was straightened and blacktopped a few years back. The other road, blacktopped too, is a rollercoaster, curvy and twisting, a conduit to a bunch of little towns that wind along the river, or just take you back home, if that's where you need to be.

When I was a little girl, my parents would take us roller skating at Snowball's on cold, wintry Saturday nights when there was nothing better to do, and mom and dad wanted to get out of the house for a while. The building itself had two separate areas then, a bar on the north side of the building where we played arcade games while my parents drank beer and visited with family and friends. The south side opened into an enormous back room with space heaters sitting scattered around on the bright orange floors, disco balls hanging from a ceiling that seemed higher than the sky to a bunch of 9-year-old girls. We felt grown up sitting on backless bar stools while we drank Fanta and popped Sprees into our orange-stained mouths. We skated around and around in circles while we sang our hearts out as the big black speakers boomed a mix from 80s hair bands and a few country classics. The two rooms are still joined by a set of stairs that were tricky to navigate in our skates and I fell more than once on my way down. The current banquet hall replaced the roller rink years ago, but the front bar is just as I remember it.

Alicia startles me as we round the final corner and the bar comes into view.

"Holy shit!" she says. "Look at the cars!"

"Oh my," I say, transitioning into song, throwing my hands up over my head while my pointer fingers shoot toward the sky like a couple of revolvers.

I gotta feeling,

That tonight's gonna be a good night

That tonight's gonna be a good, good night

A feeling, woohoo

Alicia and I are harmonizing as we pull into a front row parking spot like a couple of rock stars. As we get out of the car, there is a group with some of Alicia's friends just outside the entrance to the banquet hall who are soliciting smokers. We stop to chat a minute before I follow her inside.

The reception has already started in the banquet hall, and the bride and groom are flanked by four on each side of them at the head table, already eating. The ladies are wearing the most unusual yet lovely chartreuse green, floor-length dresses. The men are in traditional black-tie attire.

The walls are bright white and the floors a light dove gray. Lights are mingled inside white tulle, hanging from the ceilings and wrapped around trees that line the walls, which adds some color to the landscape. Directly to the right, there is a rock waterfall in the farthest corner of the room. Straight ahead, a second bar juts out from the wall just past the restrooms. The circular tables have simple white linens centered with massive floral arrangements filled with the blooms of the season in oranges and greens and reds.

As Alicia makes her way to find our table, I make a beeline directly to the bar to get a couple of beers for us when I run into an old girlfriend from high school, Dana. She's a striking woman now, with a bronzed complexion, caramel-colored eyes and hair, and always a bit of a wild one. The summer we were 13, she would come in from the country for sleepovers and we would sneak out of the daylight windows of my parents' basement after we shut out the lights, as if we were going to go to bed at 10:30. I remember how she could slide her little body right through the 10-inch opening like a human Gumby, but I was always slowed up by my taller frame and bigger backside. She would wait for me in the wet grass, urging me on like it was an Olympic event, grabbing my hand to help pull me out faster. When I was finally out, we would run like hell down to the ball field in town, free to meet boys and smoke cigarettes.

We would take the back streets, slowing down through the cemetery, neither of us afraid at all, stopping to worship a few gravestones, acknowledging the veterans and pondering why the good die young. While I was away at college, she did her fair share of partying, working as a bartender for a while and every now and then she'd be dancing on the bar at the end of the night. Now she has settled down into married life, has a couple of kids and is tied down at home.

"Hey there, lady," I say with a smile.

"Well, hey," she says. "How have you been?"

"I'm good," I lie. "How about you?"

"Yeah, me too," she says. "Busy with kids and work. You know, the usual."

"Yeah, me too," I say. "There's never a dull moment."

"Yeah, that's for sure," she says, pressing her beer to her lips.

"Well, hey, maybe talk to you later, ok?" I say.

I debate about telling her about the divorce, but I decide I don't want to ruin my buzz. She probably already knows anyway, even though she didn't say anything about it. That's life in a small town. I'm sure the rumors are flying as fast as the Shades of Grey trilogy is selling copies by now. We chat for a few more minutes and then I go to our table. I don't even want to eat. I just want to drink like a fish that's been out of water for days, even though it's only been hours.

After dinner, Alicia goes outside to have a smoke, while I sit at the table and watch the wedding party interacting with the bride and groom. The little moments between them are so sweet, innocent. The whole wedding-day-dream-becoming reality doesn't bother me as much as I thought it would. Later, when the music starts, we go back to the dance. After a couple of songs, Alicia tells me she's going outside to smoke and then get another drink. I decide to walk around and find somebody to chat with. An old friend of my brother and his wife are sitting nearby, so I stop by their table.

"Well, hey there," I say.

"Hey," he says. "How's it going, Erika? I haven't seen you in a long, long time."

"Yeah, I know," I say. "It's been a while."

"How's your hubby and the kids?" he asks.

"Well," I say, looking away. Damn, I don't want to do this right now. "It's kind of a long story."

"Well, you don't have to tell me right now if you don't want to," he says, trying to be polite. "That's ok."

I pause. I want to tell him. I just don't know how to say it. I've known him my whole life. We spent many summer nights hanging out in the neighborhood, or just listening to music or playing video games in our basement.

"We're getting a divorce, actually," I say, trying hard to not let my voice shake.

He pauses, looking surprised, clearly not knowing what to say at first.

"Oh. Well, I'm sorry to hear that," he finally says.

"Well, thanks," I say. "It's OK. It's probably better as a memory. We just had too much stuff happen."

We talk about my kids, their kids, where they are living, my new house, my parents and my brother. Then I see Alicia come around the corner from the upper bar, with a huge grin on her face. She walks right over to me.

"You have to come up front. There's someone up there you need to meet," she says, still grinning,

I look at my old friend.

"Well, I guess I better get going," I tell him, winking. "It sounds like I'm about to meet the love of my life or something."

"Well, in that case, you better get going," he says, winking back.

"I guess so," I say, smiling at him as I walk away.

"Let me know how it goes," he says.

"Oh, I will," I say. "I will."

Good grief. Here we go.

CHAPTER THREE

On the way to the bar, I'm grilling Alicia about who it is.

"Do I know him?" I ask.

"Well, he's from town, but he doesn't live around here anymore," she says.

I love a good mystery, but I still want to know who it is before I get there.

"C'mon!" I whine. "Are you going to tell me before we get up there?"

"Nope," she teases. "I want to see if you can guess who it is."

Dammit, this is going to be embarrassing, sure to bring on every ounce of social anxiety I've had since I was a kid. It all started with humanity, the blood, the guts, or the mention of a needle penetrating my skin would generate dizzying circles in my head and usually ended with it hitting whatever hard surfaced floor was under me, a hallway or a classroom or even the gym. Concussions have become a way of life for me, like an NFL quarterback who always gets up just one more time than he goes down. I'd wake up with a crowd staring at me in awe. They were always amazed at the coming alive part, of watching a girl whose head just bounced off the floor like a basketball, drool rolling down my face, my face hot and flushed, a headache starting.

For a moment, I fear the whole damn bar will probably be watching me scoping the room for whoever this mystery man is. As we're walking up the stairs, I notice some black balloons to the left, hovering in the air in the middle of the room, a party for someone who is probably older than me. When I turned 30, my family had a surprise birthday party for me, even though I suspected for months that the event was in the works. I was sent away for a day of beauty at an upscale day spa where they pampered and primped me for 8 hours like it was my job, fed me lunch, and sent me home exhausted after doing nothing at all for a day. When I got home, cars lined the dead-end street in our neighborhood and feet greeted me as the door of the garage slowly lifted to reveal family and friends, beer and food, crepe paper and black balloons. Whoever it is, they'll be glad to not have to clean up the mess that comes with having a party at home.

As we make our way up the stairs, there are feet scattered across the room, congregated toward the middle of the bar. All the bar stools are taken so we stand and wait for a bartender to come over while an old Hank Williams song blares out of the jukebox. Alicia looks at me with a smirk, then glances across the bar.

"So, do you know who it is yet?" she asks.

I turn around, shaking my head in irritation that she's doing this to me today, while I'm still in the throes of my divorce. A huge smile spreads over my face because I'm nervous, not knowing if this is some kind of stupid game that she is playing on me. I scan the room. I can feel eyes on me, over to the right, staring at me from across the room. I shift my eyes that way. There is a guy seated at the birthday table and the balloons are jumping and bouncing over his head. He is handsome, with salt and pepper hair and summer sun still baked on his skin. Our eyes meet and we're just watching each other for a moment before he tips his head back to take a drink of beer.

I turn around, declaring, "It's John Montgomery."

Alicia just smiles and says, "Yep," and she walks away.

To say that I had never met John Montgomery would be a lie. I had known him all my life. I knew most of his family and the farmhouse where he grew up. His oldest daughter was a server in my wedding. Yet, I had never been alone with him, never known him as a man. He had always seemed an old soul to me, quiet, a black sheep of his family, a little tattered, a little bruised. I never knew why. But he was handsome, no doubt about it, striking, dashing, with the perfect physical attributes for a character in a romance novel.

When I turn back around to check him out again, he is standing. He seems a little taller than I remember him, probably 6'2" and the ideal size for a quarterback. He still has the stocky build of the high school wrestler that I recall from so many years ago, when our team had a winning streak that soared over 100 and propelled us to the state tournament several years in a row. A black t-shirt bearing a cross is clinging to the curves of his upper body and jeans are hugging his lower.

John grew up here but moved away with his wife and kids in the mid-90s, just after I graduated from high school, taking a transfer with a company he'd worked for all his life. I'd heard that he went through a pretty nasty divorce a couple of years before, after his ex-wife skipped town to hook up with a 20-something-year-old, leaving him to raise his youngest daughter alone.

His older daughter was friends with Alicia when they lived here, spending lots of time with Alicia's family and my parents. They would go on long car rides, checking out the leaves in the fall with an ice cream cone in hand, out for dinner sometimes, or just to see what kind of trouble they could get into. Once in a while, they would get a little silly, a little crazy, mostly when I was off with my friends or a boyfriend.

I remember once, my parents came home laughing and giggling uncontrollably about some damn adventure they'd had earlier in the evening. When I finally got them to fess up, they told me they'd played Fire Drill at a red light in the middle of downtown. And then, just before my dad was the last to get back in the car, my uncle locked him out, with John's daughter and Alicia and watching in horror. I was a teenage girl then, and I was mortified. Needless to say, they stopped sharing their stories with me, until I was old enough to handle them. They laughed until they cried sitting at our kitchen table re-telling all their stories.

When my brother and I were in high school, my mom prepared the dinner for the German Club to help raise money for kids like us to explore northern Europe during the spring of their junior or senior year. For days before the dinner, our house wreaked of sauerkraut soup, dilled carrots, horseradish potatoes and sauerbraten. And the hard rolls were always delivered the Friday before the dinner by John. He would pick them up from a little bakery that was on his way from work. My mom would repay him with her homemade peanut brittle, some money for his gasoline, and the exchanging of beers and stories at our kitchen table.

In my high school days, I had a rare friendship with John's dad. He took a post-retirement job as a custodian in our school after working on the local county highway department crew for years. He would put treats in my locker at school and we would visit in the morning and afternoon when he took his breaks. He was the jolliest of guys, one of those folks who whistled while he worked, his eyes twinkling. After basketball games, he would grab some of us girls and make us dance with him while he hummed songs like Mel McDaniel's 'Louisiana Saturday Night,' turning us around in circles until we were dizzy and laughing. We shared the same birthday and always reminded each other when we saw one another, even after I was long gone and graduated. I would see him around town, at church or the grocery store, until he died of cancer.

I didn't see John for a long, long time until last winter when we exchanged glances at the state wrestling tournament. My family was on our way home from a vacation after spending a few days in Fort Myers watching the Minnesota Twins at spring training. As we settled into our seats that day, I could feel someone looking at me from the section just next to ours. I kept looking, but I couldn't figure out who it was. Then, our eyes met. It was John. I smiled, then turned away and looked back a few minutes later. He was still watching me. I turned away again. It was mysterious to me. I think he was divorced then, but I was married. I went back to watching the wrestling match. When I looked back a third time, he was gone. I hadn't seen him since, until tonight.

My beer is almost gone, so I order another and make my way to the banquet room. Alicia is laughing at me as I walk toward her.

"Well, thanks for leaving me up there," I complain.

"I figured you'd want to come back down here to talk anyway," she says.

"Damn, he is hot," I say, but that doesn't even begin to describe it for me.

"Yep," she says, taking a swig of her beer. "Pretty much."

We stand in the back by the bar, watching people dancing, talking about John's daughters, a little bit of the divorce drama, and my strategy for meeting him. Alicia says it will be easy, but I'm not so sure. We dance a couple of songs with the new bride and then head back up to the front bar to get another can of liquid courage because I know I'm going to need it. The bar has cleared out a little now so Alicia takes a seat on an open bar stool. I crack my beer as I walk around to the other side of the bar to get another look at John. His niece and nephew are standing next to him. Then a few minutes later, she strolls over to the bar by us.

"Hey there, ladies," Angie says as she approaches. "Are you having fun?"

"Hell, yeah. Just got done dancing to 'I Knew the Bride,'" Alicia says. "Have you been back there to the dance?"

"No, I've been hanging out up here, babysitting my husband so he doesn't get too out of hand," she says, winking.

While they're chatting, I'm glancing back and forth between the two ladies and John, while he's talking to Angie's husband.

Suddenly, he stands up and starts walking around his table toward the bar.

"Erika?" Alicia says, trying to get my attention. "Are you listening?"

"What?" I ask, lost in the moment of it, turning to her. "What?"

"Do you want something more to drink?" she asks, annoyed with me for ignoring her. "I'm buying."

I lift my bottle of beer off the bar and tilt it sideways, still watching John.

"No," I say. "I'm good."

Thankfully, John stops to chat with a guy from town so I've got another minute to figure out what the hell I'm going to say if he comes over here. The beer in his hand is almost empty. I want to be suave, smooth, offer to buy him a drink, but I just lose my cool, standing there awkwardly watching him as he orders a Jeremiah Sweet Tea. He flashes his brilliant white smile at us, then looks at his niece.

"Erika," Angie says, turning to me with a huge grin. "Have you met John?"

"Hey," I say. "How's it goin'?"

Angie and Alicia start walking away from the bar toward the banquet hall, leaving John and me alone. Our deep green eyes meet. I've known him all my life but I feel like this is different. I'm a grown woman, single, trying to move on from my divorce. If nothing else, he'd be a great one to add to my list.

"I'm great," he says. "How 'bout you?"

"Me too," I say.

Right now, in this very moment, it's the truth. I'm better than good, actually. I'm elated, thrilled, horny. I don't want to sound cocky, and I'm nervous. But my heart is breaking for the fact that my marriage of 13 years is ending, and I know I have a long road ahead of me. I feel like I've got to slow this moment down, just a bit. On that note, I grab my drink, turn around and start walking away, leaving John standing at the bar. I have no idea where I'm going, but that was just hot enough to fry the eggs that I'd like to whip him up for breakfast tomorrow. I might even offer him some bacon to go with it.

I head straight for the banquet room to hunt down Alicia. She is standing by the bar talking to her best high school friend, Catherine. She looks a little surprised to see me.

"What are you doing down here?" she asks. "You're supposed to be up in the bar talking to John."

"I couldn't stay. I'm nervous," I tell her. "I don't know. He just makes me nervous."

"Who are we talking about?" her friend Catherine asks.

At first I don't want to tell her. I don't want all kinds of stories started because I just met the guy. Good grief, I've got to play it cool.

"John Montgomery," Alicia tells her, laughing, her eyes lighting up.

"Oh, he is so handsome," Catherine says.

"Oh, I know. I just really met him for the first time, and I had to walk away because I didn't know what to say after 'hello' and 'I'm good,'" I say.

They're both bent over, laughing hysterically at my honesty.

"Don't laugh at me," I say, my face turning to the scowl that I inherited from my mom's side of the family.

"That doesn't sound anything like you to be nervous around a man," Alicia says. "What the hell."

"I know," I say. "I don't know what it is. He's older than me. Maybe that's it."

Alicia looks at me with bent eyebrows.

"No way," she says, putting one of her hands on my back and pushing me toward the door. "Get back up there and find a way to talk to him. He doesn't come around very often and he's here tonight so you better make it a good one."

I look at Alicia, then at Catherine, then back to Alicia. They don't say anything. They're waiting for me to put on my big girl panties and march right back up to the bar and get something started with John. I tilt my head back and slam my beer, just about wiping out on a wet spot on the floor as I'm trying to shake my ass and flip my hair in a dramatic moment. I turn around and Alicia and Catherine are watching me, roaring with laughter.

When I get back up front, I order another beer and glance around the room for John. I don't see him, but some of his family is still sitting at the table with the balloons so I figure he's got to be around here somewhere. My old friend Dana is holding up the bar so I pull up a seat next to her.

"Hey there," I say.

"Hey, you need a beer?" she asks.

"Sure," I say.

"Hey, can you get Erika a beer?" she hollers over to one of the bartenders, who brings a beer and sets it in front of me. "Can you just put it on our tab?"

"So I guess you've probably heard about my divorce, huh?" I ask.

"Actually, yeah, I heard some rumblings about it last weekend, but I didn't know if it was true," she confirms.

"Yeah, it is," I tell her. "I bought a house a few weeks ago, and the paperwork will be filed with the county any day now. Hopefully it won't take long."

"How long does it usually take?" she asks.

"I don't know, 3 maybe 4 months," I say. "I just hope it's over by Christmas."

"Yeah, I can't imagine," she says. "I'm sorry you're going through that."

"It's OK," I say. "I just feel bad for my kids right now. It's going to be rough for them."

Toward the end of our conversation, John walks in from outside. I can't take my eyes off him. He walks over and stands at the other end of the bar, waiting for the bartender to serve him. I catch him glancing at me and we both smile. My friend excuses herself and walks away, and I'm standing there alone, feeling like an idiot. I'm hoping that he'll come a little closer, and then he does.

"So, what are you doing home this weekend?" I ask, trying to make small talk.

"Well, it's my sister's birthday party down here tonight so I figured I better come home for it," he says. "It was a good day for a drive."

"Yeah, definitely, a beautiful day for a wedding too," I throw back. "I went out and got drunk last night, slept in until noon, then got up and started getting ready to come here. I kind of wasted the day."

"I got a new car a few weeks ago," he says. "So I decided to get in the car and go. I got pulled over on the way down."

"You're kidding me?" I say. "Did you get a ticket?"

"No," he says. "He told me he'd let me down easy this time."

"Lucky," I say. "That never happens to me. Maybe we can go for a ride sometime?"

He pauses and takes a drink.

"What about now?" he asks, his smile beaming.

"Are you kidding me?" I ask.

"No, let's go if you want to," he says, putting his hands at his waist like I'm wasting time.

"OK, let's go," I say.

He turns and heads toward the door, and I follow him, turning back to wink at Alicia as we walk out of the bar. The only thing that could possibly have made the moment any better is if he was holding my hand. And then, when we get outside, he does.

CHAPTER FOUR

From across the parking lot, I see a sleek black Chevy Camaro parked right in front of the building. My heart is humming with the idea of going somewhere in this hot car with a man who already completely turns me on. I wonder for a moment if I'll be able to control myself, but decide to not worry about it, just to let things happen. I remind myself of the summer I had, of the lonely nights, of the fights with my ex, the day he told me he wanted a divorce. I remind myself that I deserve to be happy, that I deserve to have a little fun, even if only for one night. As we get closer to the car, he walks around to the passenger side and opens the door for me. Like it's not cool enough to be going for a drive with him somewhere. Now, he's tugging at my heart strings, or maybe it's more like my black lace thong. There is a crowd of smokers standing outside the bar gawking at us.

"Well, thank you, sir," I tell him, smiling as I move past him, slightly grazing his shirt. I slide my ass onto the black leather seat.

He just smiles. He's a man of few words. I love it. It's the best kind of chemistry. He moves around the other side of the car, opens the door and slides into his seat. I'm watching his strong, thick legs as he adjusts his jeans. My, oh my, I'd like to have a feel of those. He looks over at me, catching me gazing at his legs. He starts the car, and the music comes on, blaring. I laugh out loud because that's exactly what it's like when I get in my own car.

"Sorry," he says.

"No problem," I tell him. laughing. "I like it."

He grabs the volume knob and turns it down a little. As we pull out of the parking spot, most of the crowd outside is still watching us. This will be a great story for the local headlines tomorrow morning, I'm sure.

"So, can you name the song?" he asks.

Now I'm blown away. Maybe he loves music as much as I do. I can't distinguish the song right away, so I sit there listening through the first few bars, until the voices begin. Just when I think it's not going to come to me and I'm about ready to give up, a huge smile comes over my face.

"'Broken Wings,'" I say, looking at him.

"And the artist?" he asks.

"Hmm, just wait," I say. "I know it's an 80s hair band. Just give me a second."

The car comes to a stop at the end of the driveway, where the gravel meets the asphalt. He hits the gas and the tires squeal as we roll out on to the county road. I have no idea where we are going, and I really don't even care. I realize that I don't know much about John at all, but I feel so comfortable, so safe. I feel like I am doing exactly what I'm supposed to be doing, like this is exactly what is supposed to happen to me tonight. I turn to him and our eyes meet.

"'Mister, Mister,'" I say, figuring he'll be surprised.

"I'm impressed," he says, smiling.

He grabs the radio knob to turn up the volume as the car veers sharply to the left, heading north away from the bar. He looks over at me as the car accelerates and we're flying down the back country road. I turn the window down hoping it will fix the sweaty mess I made while I was dancing. I lean my head out the window, enjoying the wind on my face. I feel so free, like a dog riding shotgun on a hot summer day with its tongue flapping in the breeze. I pull my head back inside and try to re-organize my head of curls. I grab for the knob on the radio to turn it down again.

"I was sorry to hear about your dad. I didn't make it to the funeral, but I was sad to hear that he died." I tell him, my voice soft. "He was a great man. We had the best time together back when I was in high school. He was always trying to cheer me up from my sorrows of the day."

"Thanks, it was tough," he says, looking over at me.

"God, it must have been hard," I say, my voice growing thick, trying not to cry. "My dad is one of my best friends. I can't imagine losing him."

"I was coming home alone every weekend, leaving work early on Fridays and going back late on Monday nights so that I could be with him as much as possible. Yeah, and we were having marriage problems at the time too, so that didn't make it any easier," he says. "She was gone every weekend partying and I was coming home."

"Wow," I say. "That's not cool. Were you there when he died?"

"No," he says. "I was on my way."

He doesn't look at me anymore while we're talking about it. I figure it's hard for him so I change the subject.

"So, how long have you been divorced now?" I ask.

"A couple of years now," he says. "It was a mess."

"Mine too," I say. "After 1500 bucks and three hours of mediation, it was over."

"Wow, that was fast," he says, his eyebrows raising. "And cheap."

We both laugh. I can just about imagine what his cost him.

"Now I just have to wait for it to be final I guess. Hopefully by the end of the year," I say.

It's my turn to have a change of subjects now. We're both quiet, but it's not awkward at all. The introvert in me just wants to say nothing at all, just be there, enjoy the moment. A few miles down the road, I move my hand over to rest on his leg, then lean into him and kiss him on the cheek. His cologne is so subtle, so barely noticeable that it turns me on.

"Hmm, you smell amazing," I say.

He immediately slows the car down then and pulls it into a field drive that leads to a quarry. He puts the car in park and turns off the headlights. There is light beaming from a pole that sits toward the back of the quarry, about 100 yards away. I look out my window, admiring the blackest night sky with stars scattered. I turn back around to find John staring at me.

"What?" I ask, trying to not smile but not able to help myself.

"Nothing," he says, smiling back, great confidence in his face.

I lean in closer to him and put my hand on his leg again. He looks toward me, a little surprised, and then he leans in a little closer. We sit there, motionless, for just a few seconds, but it feels like forever, waiting for him to kiss me. Finally, I can't stand it anymore.

"Are you going to kiss me or what?" I ask, trying to not giggle.

And without saying anything at all, he leans in and softly kisses me on the cheek and backs away. Well, that's not exactly what I had in mind. I take my hand off his leg and put it on the side of his face, pulling him back toward me. His skin is soft, smooth. I love a man who shaves every day. I give him the kiss that I was expecting, long and wet and deep. He kisses me back. We sit there for a few minutes just exchanging soft kisses, me starting up a little bit harder, pushing my face into him. I open my eyes, looking at him while we're kissing. I know that it's totally against the rules, but I can't help it. It's just the way I am. Then he opens his too, and we're watching each other, both smiling. He's trying to be a gentleman and I won't let him.

I am already wet. I take my hand from his face and move it down his shirt to his jeans. He's slightly hard, but not all the way there. It turns me on knowing he's so into this. I undo the button on his jeans, and tug at his zipper. It sticks halfway down, and I have to use my other hand to get it all the way. I reach inside his jeans, trying to get to his concrete cock, but unfortunately, he's not going to make it easy for me. He's got some sort of spandex contraption on under his jeans. I grab hastily at the waistband and pull it down below his penis where I can finally get my hands on him. Now he's hard. I smile as I lift my ass out of the seat and lean over the center console to wrap my lips around him. He's huge, way bigger than my ex, even bigger than my first sexual escapade a few weeks ago. John is even longer and thicker. But he's no challenge for me. I already know that I'll fit all of him in my mouth, but I tease him a little and play with the tip before moving down his shaft. He moans but says nothing. I love that too. He grabs at the side of his chair to lean the seat back. It jerks then falls until it hits the backseat.

I go all the way down on him then, and he moans. I take all of him in my mouth and hold it there. He grabs the back of my head and pushes my mouth onto him, as far as I can go. I start slowly moving up and down, then move faster until he's wet. He is moving his hips into me then, and we've got a rhythm together for a few minutes. I pull away and look up at him.

"Wow, are you ever good at that," he tells me.

"Well, thanks," I reply, pride in my voice.

It's not the first blowjob I've ever given, but it's the first to someone other than my husband. My legs are crossed and I'm laying on my left side, leaning toward him. He moves his hands over me now. The dress I'm wearing has a long slit in the short skirt. He reaches his hand inside the top where it crosses and meets in the middle, running his hand over my black lace bra, then pulling the fabric down and hovering his thumb over my nipple. I'm breathing heavier now, excited from the moment. He rolls my nipple between his thumb and forefinger until it hardens. Soon his other hand is inside my dress, rubbing the other nipple. He moves his other hand down my dress and pushes my skirt open at the slit to uncover my black lace thong. He grabs it and moves it sideways. Then he slides his hand over me, brushing against my skin. I hate being quiet but I've gotten used to it with three kids at home. Out here in the boondocks, it turns me on that I don't have to be.

He slides his middle finger over my clit. I love that middle finger thing. It's bigger than the others, and better than the thumb. He rubs back and forth over it, back and forth, back and forth. Then he slips it inside me. I move my hips down off the seat so he can press it all the way inside me. Oh, he is so deep.

"I want to do that again," I whisper.

He pulls his finger out of me and moves his hand around to grab my ass. As I start to bend over again toward him, he pulls me up.

"Let's get out of the car," he says.

I answer by grabbing the handle on the door. I step out and stumble, forgetting I'm wearing high heels. I debate about taking them off, but figure leaving them on will be sexier. If there wasn't gravel under my feet, they'd be gone. I push my dress down but leave my top wide open and my tits half hanging out. My hair is a damn mess, the curls frizzed out from hanging my head out the window on the drive. As I walk around to John's side of the car, I throw my hands in my hair, trying to tame it down. I want to look like a sex kitten for the night instead of an All-American girl.

John is standing on the other side of the car, leaning into the hood. His pants are hanging wide open, his briefs holding at the middle of his penis, looking damn sexy. As I walk toward him, I can't help but laugh at how crazy this is.

"What?" he asks, his face confused.

I just smile and reply by grabbing the sides of his face and kissing him hard. Then I grab his boxer briefs and jeans and push them down to his knees, giving his penis a kiss on the way. His pants are skimming the ground and I laugh to myself. It reminds me of when I was 16 and I worked at the local drive-in on the outskirts of town. It was a Friday afternoon, a beautiful, hot summer day, somewhere between the lunch rush and the late afternoon swimming rats on their way home from the pool. The cook and I were all alone in the kitchen. He flirted with me persistently and asked me out about every other week. He was standing back by the fryer, and I was up front closer to the order peephole. I was leaning against the counter, both hands occupied by a delicious pineapple sundae, my personal favorite. As I was slurping some ice cream backwards off the spoon, he came around from behind me, grabbed my shorts, and dropped them to the ground, panties and all. It was unstoppable with the sundae in my hand. I was mortified, but I calmly set down my sundae, pulled up my shorts and panties, then took the kitchen towel and relentlessly beat him across the head until he begged me to stop. Stupid boy.

I'm still giggling when John grips me under my arms and pulls me back up to meet his face, kissing me, then grabbing my dress and lifting it to my waist. My ass is brushing against the side of the car, leaving wet marks across the hood. He grabs my thong and pushes it sideways again. I lean back against the car. He picks me up under one side of my ass and then lowers himself a little so that our bodies are even. He pushes himself inside, halfway, then he gives me all of him. I am so wet, that's all it takes.

"God damn," I say. "That feels fantastic."

He grabs me behind my neck to keep me from falling backwards over the car, pulling me closer to him. He starts thrusting into me, harder and faster for a few minutes, and then he slows down. I'm watching his face. He closes his eyes for little moments and then he opens them and looks at me. It feels so natural with him, like we just fit. I'd had great sex during my marriage, but it was nothing like this. I put my hands under his shirt, and then move them over his chest and stomach. He has hard, strong muscles, with messy salt and pepper curls on his chest.

"I love it," I say, smiling.

Suddenly, toward the road I see headlights approaching and a car flies by, driving fast and then hitting the brakes as it rounds the corner past the quarry. John stops altogether and watches the car as it rolls by. It keeps moving down the road, but now we're both freaked out.

"We better get heading back," he says, pulling away from me.

"Damn," I say, breathlessly. "Are you kidding me? When are we going to finish this?"

"Maybe later," he says, teasing me with a smile.

Our eyes are locked as he steps backwards and grabs for the handle on the car door. I make my way around the other side of the car as John watches me.

What the hell. All I can think about is that he damn well better follow through.

When we get back in the car, the radio is booming Poison's, "Talk Dirty to Me" when John turns over the ignition. Oh, I will, believe me. He puts the car in drive and before we're even out of the quarry, I lean across the seat and I'm all over him again. He accelerates fast and we're racing down the road. I cannot keep my mouth off of him. His silence turns me on, along with the blaring dirty talk. He reaches across my body and slips his hand inside my dress. I am gyrating to the music, like he's a guitar player strumming the sweetest damn song. I grab at my thong and push it over my knees, down to the floor, then fling it out the window, figuring I'm not going to need it anymore tonight anyway.

Before I know it, we're slowing down to round the corner to turn into the driveway of the bar. I back away from him, tuck my boobs back into my bra, and slide my dress down just before a crowd of smokers standing in front of the bar can get a peepshow as we pull into a parking spot.

"So, how about if I go in the back door and you go in the front?" I say, leaning in for a kiss. "We don't need any rumors starting, right?"

"Yeah," he says. "Sure."

I open the car door and start walking haphazardly across the gravel in my peep-toe heels toward the back entrance of the banquet room while John is still standing at the car. After I fling open the door, I turn to watch him as he walks into the entrance of the bar. Mmm, was that ever fun.

CHAPTER FIVE

As I walk into the banquet room, I see Alicia standing at the bar. She rushes over to me with Catherine following her.

"Where in the hell have you been?" Alicia asks.

"I just went for a drive with John," I tell her, a huge grin coming over my face.

"Yeah, whatever," she says. "I'll bet you were on a drive."

"We were," I say. "I'm not kidding. We drove down to the quarry and just sat there and talked. It was nice."

"Well, what's with the red shit all over your neck?" she asks.

"What do you mean?" I ask.

"You've got red blotchy skin," she says, still wanting an explanation.

"Well, it's cold outside," I say, trying to explain them away and do it without a smile.

"Well, if it was just a drive, then why were you outside?" she asks.

"I had the window down," I say. "And I touch my neck when I'm nervous."

She looks at me, then at Catherine, and back at me. I just can't stop smiling.

"Whatever," she says. "You're such a liar."

I'm smiling as I walk away, and head back up to the bar where I hope John will be waiting for me.

When I get to the bar, John is ordering a drink. It turns me on thinking about the sex we just had on the side of his car. I smile.

"You want something to drink?" he asks.

"Sure, I'll take a beer," I say.

He orders my favorite without even asking. What kind of man knows a woman's beer preference on the first night? Soon, John's niece makes her way from the dance floor through the crowd of people and over to us.

"Where've you two been?" she asks, grinning.

I look at John, waiting for him to answer since she's his family and I already got a heckling from Alicia.

"Just on a drive," he tells her.

"Pretty long drive, don't ya think?" she asks.

John looks over at me and says, "Well, we got lost on a back road."

"Yeah, whatever," she says. "I bet."

I love it. He grew up taking the back roads that wind around our little existence in the boondocks and I'm certain that she knows him better than that, but she leaves it alone. In the moment, I'm wondering if he went to the bathroom and washed his hands when he got back in the bar. If not, I'm totally turned on. Over our heads, Flo Rida's "Low" starts booming. Alicia comes over from the other end of the bar and grabs my hand, pulling me out to the dance floor. As we're dancing, I watch John across the room. He moves a little closer to the floor, staring between my legs as I go down to the floor. On my way back up, I stumble, drunk. He takes a drink of his beer, still staring at me. He stands there and watches me go up and down until the song is over. I grab Alicia and give her a long hug.

"So, did you have fun with John?" she asks.

"Umm, yeah," I say. "I did. I really did," my face brightening when I say it.

"Well, let's get some shots to celebrate," she says, heading toward the bar as I follow her.

John, Angie and Dana are all standing at the bar together when we get there. Alicia orders up five shots for us. As we hold up our glasses, I shout out a stupid little toast that we always overused in college.

Here's to you

And here's to me

The best of friends we'll always be

And if we ever disagree

The fuck with you and here's to me

As it spills out of my mouth, it reminds me of the "best friend" who at present is likely spending the night sleeping in my old bed and fucking my husband. How lovely. With that, I decide we need another shot.

"Five more, please," I shout to the bartender, throwing a twenty out on the bar.

Everybody looks at me like I'm crazy, like I've had enough. As the bartender sets them down, I push them out to my companions.

"Let's do that one again," I say, throwing the shot into the air, winking at John as I tip it back.

I repeat the best friend toast, but this time, it doesn't hurt as badly. I guess the alcohol is kicking in. Alicia sets down her glass and grabs her camera out of her purse, moving behind the bar to get a picture of the rest of us.

"Smile," she shouts from the other side of the bar.

She takes the picture and then leans over the bar to show us the shot. My tits are hanging out, but what the hell. I immediately wonder if John and I could look any more perfect together, then I realize how nauseating that is. As he steps away to move closer to the table where his family is sitting, he brushes against me, teasing me with his touch. I get another beer and shake my ass to a few more songs before last call. I catch John glancing my way and we hold our stare for a moment. As the bar starts clearing out, a few of us, including John and I, are standing around chatting. It's 1 in the morning, and I get the bright idea to announce that I'm having an after bar. It's perfect though, since I spent Friday afternoon cleaning my house and I just filled my fridge with beer.

"Well, who can come over?" Alicia asks.

"Whoever," I say. "It doesn't matter to me. I just got a bunch of beer and I think I've got some pizzas in the freezer. Come on over," I say to the group.

I turn to John to give him a personal invitation.

"Are you coming?" I ask.

"Sure," he says. "But only if you're riding with me."

"Absolutely," I say, smiling.

Hell yes, I am definitely riding you. I mean, riding with you.

As we're walking out of the bar, I push open the door and John puts his hand on my back. I turn and look at him. I feel like I already know him somehow. I trust him. I guess I should since I just went for a ride in his car and had sex with him under the stars. As we head to his car, I holler to Alicia to just let herself into my house when she gets there. I've got a feeling she's probably going to beat us there. We hop in his car and he hesitates a few minutes before he puts the car in drive. Then I realize that he's letting everyone else leave before we take off.

We barely get out of the driveway of the bar and I'm leaning across the seat, kissing his neck, my hands all over him, rubbing his penis, down his legs. He puts his hand on my leg and moves it up under my dress. This time my panties are gone and he goes directly for the goods. I can't stand having his hands all over me and not doing something more to him so I unbutton his pants and thrust my hand inside. He's already hard. I lean across the seat and go down on him, gently sucking the tip of his manhood as he moans. I have no idea how far we've driven when he starts slowing down then takes a left. As I pick my head up and look around, it feels like we're in the middle of a corn field. He's still got his hands on me as he pulls me into him and kisses me, softly now.

"Let's get out of the car," I whisper, reaching for the door.

I watch as he gets out and walks to the back of the car, holding his pants up. I meet him at the middle of the tailgate.

"How 'bout right here," he says, placing his hands on the back of the car.

"Sure," I say, moving closer and kissing him.

John's pants slide down his legs, landing on the cold, wet ground. He puts his hands under my ass and helps me up on the tailgate. I lay back, the car wet from the humidity in the air. It's cold, but it feels good on my back. It's slippery too. John lowers his pants, and they fall to the ground. Hopefully it's not muddy wherever the hell we are, or he's going to look like a moron when we get back to my house. I'm not as wet as I was before. He takes a little longer to slip inside me, but then his tempo builds and we are slamming against each other. He is holding my legs up in the air, bracing

me there so I don't slip on the wet car.

"Let's go to your house," he says, suggesting we can finish there.

He grabs my hands and helps me down from the tailgate. My legs are weak from him holding them over my head. I stumble, partly because my feet are asleep and partly because I'm wasted. I push my dress back down and get back in the car. As he's backing the car on to the highway, he slows, and leans in and kisses me gently.

"I'm hungry," I tell him.

"Me too," he says.

And I'm not talking about pizza, but I figure he probably isn't either.

CHAPTER SIX

When we get to my house, the party has already started. Alicia brought some beer up from the basement, and there are people out on the deck smoking. John and I stand in the kitchen together when they come inside. I start the oven and throw the pizzas in.

"Where have you two been?" Catherine asks.

"We took the back roads home," I say slurring.

"Well, you must have gotten lost on the way, huh?" she says.

"Yeah, something like that," I say, smiling at John, then at her.

One of Alicia's friends asks if he can have a tour of my house.

"Sure," I say, looking at John and putting my hand on his arm. "Be right back, OK?"

"Sure," he says.

I give her friend a tour of my house, first the upstairs, then down to the basement. We're down there for a few minutes when I hear the timer on the oven go off. We head back upstairs for some pizza. When we get upstairs, Alicia is taking the pizza out of the oven and I throw another one in right behind her. When we finish the first pizza, the rest of the group heads out to the deck to smoke again. John and I are standing alone in the kitchen, so I step a little closer to him and try to kiss him, but he backs away.

"What's the matter?" I ask.

"Nothing," he says, looking out toward the deck.

"Well, let's go to my bedroom then," I say.

I grab his hand and lead him that way. I shut the door behind us and pull him in close to me, kissing him hard. When I move my hand down his pants, he's already hard again. I think it might be my lucky day. I push him down on the bed and he lifts my dress to my waist. I undo the button on his pants, for the third time tonight. I grab his jeans by the belt loops and slowly tug them off. By now, he's completely hard. I mount him and ease him into me. God, I can feel all of him this way. It feels amazing. I start moving up and down as he's watching me. Then he moves his hands inside my bra and strokes my tits while I ride him. I can hear voices outside. They sound close to the window so I get off and close the blinds. I have no idea what they just saw but I'm sure it was some kind of show.

When I get back to John, he's rock hard and watching me. I climb back on and push him inside me. I move over him in a rhythm for a few minutes. The bed is noisy, squeaking with every gyration. A clamor when I move one way and a clatter when I move the other. He grabs me at the hips and shoves me into him, not hard, but rhythmically.

"Are you close," I ask.

"Yeah, close," he says.

I move faster over him. He closes his eyes and then I know. I slow down and push him all the way into me. A few seconds later, he is coming, quietly, eyes closed, his hands on the side of the bed. In that moment, I already know that I want to have sex with him when I'm sober. After he finishes, I lay there on top of him for a few minutes. Then he brings his wrist up to his face.

"Shit," he says. "It's 3:15. I gotta get going."

"Don't you want to stay?" I ask, already knowing that he won't.

"I want to, but I can't," he says. "Not tonight. I'm staying at my parent's house and my mom will be up waiting for me."

We lay there a minute and then he slowly pushes me off of him. He buttons his pants as I stand there watching him. I grab my bathrobe and throw it on so I can walk him out. He comes closer and gives me a kiss, then opens the door to my bedroom. When we walk into the living room, everyone else is standing in the kitchen.

"What the hell were you two doing?" Alicia asks, smiling.

I give her the shut-your-damn-mouth look as John and I head toward the mudroom, then through the garage to his car. When he grabs the car door to open it, I want to ask him to stay again, but I don't. It's cold in the September night, standing in my bathrobe, my hard nipples showing through the front, in bare feet and crazy curly hair.

"You wanna give me your number?" he asks, with his phone in his hand.

"Yeah, sure," I say, as I rattle it off and he enters it. "Are you on Facebook?"

"Yeah," he confirms. "Every now and then."

"I'll friend you tomorrow, OK?" I tell him.

"Sounds good," he says.

I'm standing by the door of the car as we lean into each other for one last kiss. Then he bends down and gets in his car.

"Drive safe," I say, leaning in through the window for the real last kiss. "Text me when you get home, OK?"

"I will," he says.

He turns the ignition on the hot little sports car, backs down the driveway and heads down my street. I wonder if he'll call, but I know I'll be OK if he doesn't. I turn around and walk back toward the house. Happy girl has got to be written all over my face.

When I get back in the house, my friends are all over me. I just want to play it cool right now, so I say nothing, but 15 minutes after John is gone I've still got this happy girl thing going on. I kick the rest of the guys out just before 4 that morning. Alicia, Catherine and a few of their friends all spend the night, scattered throughout my house. When I head to my bedroom to finally sleep, I have a text message on my phone. It's from a number I don't recognize.

Already home

It's John. I want to say 'me too'. I feel like I am already home too.

CHAPTER SEVEN

In the morning, I wake to muffled voices in the living room. When I check my phone, it's 9:30. I have a brutal headache and I just want to sleep, but I roll out of bed to see who's up and what's going on. Everybody but me is sitting in the living room, debriefing on the events from last night.

"Oh, there she is, the little tramp," one says.

"What?" I say, astonished.

I've never been called a tramp in my life, at least not to my face. And who's calling the kettle black anyway?

"So are you going to tell us what happened with you and John last night when you disappeared from the bar?" Catherine asks.

"I already told you guys," I say. "We just went for a drive."

"Well, that was an awfully long drive if you ask me," Alicia chimes in.

I say nothing.

"So, what about you girls," I say. "Did anybody else get lucky last night?"

"What do you mean, anybody else?" Catherine asks, laughing.

I didn't even realize I gave myself away.

"Oh, shit," I say. "So much for secrets."

"All right, lady," Catherine says. "Spill it."

They look at each other and then back at me. I start blushing. Oh, I figure what the hell. I tell them everything, the sex at the quarry, on the tailgate, in my bedroom. They all give me high fives. I feel like I've got a young school girl look on my face that I'll never be able to wash off. In fact, I'm not even sure that I want to. I just had one of the most amazing nights of my life and I really just want to tell the whole damn world.

After the ladies leave that morning, I go for a walk, trying to sweat out the demons from the night before. When I get home, I go back to bed until late afternoon. When I wake up, I get on Facebook and send a friend request to John. I make dinner, mow the lawn, and settle in with a bowl of popcorn and a book.

At 7:30, my phone starts ringing. I figure it's probably one of the kids just wanting to chat, but it's John. Immediately my hands start sweating, my heart racing. I'm shocked that he's calling me so soon. I figured he would give it a couple of days, or I might never hear from him again.

"Hey there," I say, answering on the third ring.

"Hey," he says. "How are you?"

"I'm pretty good. A little hungover," I say. "What about you?"

"Not too bad," he says.

His voice sounds so different over the phone, more masculine or rugged or something. I pause for a moment, trying to figure out what to say.

"So, how was your drive back?" I ask, laying down on my bed so I can sit still and concentrate.

"Long, boring," he says.

"I can imagine," I say. "I like to get in the car and drive, just go somewhere."

"I used to," he says. "But after driving back and forth for 15 years, I've kinda gotten tired of it."

"Yeah, that's understandable," I say. "So, what did you do all day?"

"Well, I got home early afternoon, watched some football and then I went for a bike ride," he says.

"You mean like motorcycle?" I ask.

"Yeah, I bought a bike last summer, a Harley," he says.

"Do you wear a helmet?" I ask.

"No, I don't even own one," he says. "So, what did you to today?"

"I went for a walk, thought it would make me feel better, but then I slept the rest of the day," I admit. "I was very lazy."

"That's alright every once in a while," he says.

"But then I mowed the lawn and made dinner," I tell him. "So that was good."

"So when do your kids come home?" he asks.

"Tomorrow," I say. "They'll be back tomorrow."

"And how old are they?" he asks.

"My oldest son is 13. My youngest is 9, and my daughter is 6," I tell him.

"And how are they doing with all of this?" he asks.

"Oh, fine for now," I tell him. "They don't really know what's about to hit them though."

"What do you mean?" he asks.

"Well, my ex has probably been fucking my best friend for a while now," I say. "And her daughter is our goddaughter, and her ex is my husband's best friend, so it's going to make for a pretty big mess."

"Oh, I see," he says. "I'm sorry to hear that."

"Yeah, I've got a little bit of baggage," I say.

"Hey, me too," he says. "Everybody does, right?"

"Yeah, I guess," I say, unsure because I'm just kind of getting used to mine.

"Hey, can I call you right back?" he asks. "I need to take another call."

"Yeah, sure," I say. "And if you don't, that's alright too. Talk to you soon."

I roll off the bed so that I don't sit and stare at the phone until he calls back. I start doing planks then leg kicks. Now that I'm a single woman, I have a new fascination with working out. It helps relieve stress, taking out the frustrations of my life with a side kick to the groin of some imaginary man. Working out and swearing, those are my vices these days. About ten minutes later, I am pleasantly surprised when John's number shows up on my phone again.

"Hey," I say. "Is everything alright?"

"Yeah, it was my daughter," he says. "She just needed some advice on some college stuff."

"Well, that's cool," I say. "What year is she?"

"She's a sophomore," he tells me.

I start thinking about my own college experience at a small, private Catholic school in the middle of the state. Of all my years in college, my sophomore year was by far the best. I lived in an apartment on campus, with six other women. I lived in a triple on the main level, and there were two doubles up a flight of stairs. Seven women sharing one bathroom is not always the most pleasant experience in life, but we made it through with very few arguments, at least that's how I remember it.

I chose the college after my first high school boyfriend attended the school while I dated him in my sophomore year in high school. I visited there just one once with his parents when they dropped him off in the fall of his first year. We broke up the next summer and my heart was broken for most of the 11th grade, but I knew it was where I wanted to go anyway.

When he came home for Christmas during that year that we dated, he surprised me in my health class when he showed up dressed as a present, red paper donning holly and ivy skillfully taped around a box, the worst wrapping job ever, but sweet just the same. He wore red tights and sang me a holiday tune that in the moment I thought I would never forget, but for the life of me I cannot remember it now.

He was perfect as far as boyfriends go. It reminds me of an old t-shirt I bought after we broke up. It had a gingerbread man on it, and it said, "The perfect boyfriend. He's quiet. He's sweet. And if he gives you any crap, you can bite his head off." I wore it everywhere, volleyball and basketball practices, the grocery store, just at home with a pair of my brothers' boxers rolled at the waist. I suppose it was my way of telling the other guys to back off for a while. My first boyfriend wasn't anything like the t-shirt.

We would talk on the phone for hours, me laying on the floor of my parents' basement, twirling the long, black phone cord around my fingers with my feet stuck to the full-length mirror that hung at the end of the hallway by the bathroom. It was like a dream for me to carry on a conversation with a boy, about big things or little things, just anything at all. Sometimes he would even argue with me, which always made me like him more, make me want to kiss him right through the phone. He was intellectual, yet we talked about some of the stupidest damn things, dog shit, lawn mowing, boogers.

He would pick me up in his parents' turquoise Ford Mustang convertible and we would head to the big city and cruise up and down Broadway for hours, stopping at Taco Bell or McDonald's along the way. When I got him home to my parents' basement, I would be all over him, begging him to let me do whatever I wanted to him, but he never did. He's the only reason I didn't have sex before I was 18. He had the audacity to say no to me.

College was good to me, and I ended up with only $22,000 in debt, partly because I had blue collar parents whose incomes were nothing compared to some of the parents of the friends that I made while I was there. But I worked 3 jobs too, one in the Development Office, calling and sending correspondence to alumni and benefactors with millions of dollars they wanted to donate to the college. Another in the writing lab, where I helped other students put together papers for their dreaded English class, the horror of one more paper all over their face when they walked through the door. The last, a member of the college newspaper staff, where I started out as a staff writer and worked my way up to the senior editor position my senior year. I left abruptly and secretly the December of my senior year to escape the shame and judgment of being pregnant on campus at an all-women's Catholic college.

I decide to give John the condensed version of my college story, knowing that he probably started working to support the family life that started for him at 19.

"I started out as an English major, with an emphasis in writing," I say. "But after I aced most of the classes, I switched over to communications. I took a class in journalism, and I was hooked. I made history when I got an 'A' on the first assignment in Journalism 101. My instructor was a hard ass too."

"Wow, that's amazing," he says.

Now I feel like it's maybe the stupidest thing I've said, ever.

"So, what's your favorite color underwear?" I ask, making a major conversation changer.

When it leaves my mouth, I feel like I should have said 'panty,' but it's a little late now. Panties, underwear, it's the thought that counts. The thought of a woman's panties is always a good one for a man like John.

"Oh, I don't know," he says, laughing, pausing for a moment. "I guess it would have to be pink."

"Hmm," I say. "Pink is a good choice. I like that."

"Or, maybe nothing," he says.

"Yeah, nothing is good too," I say, smiling.

I want to wink but we're on the phone.

"So, when are you coming around again?" I ask.

"I don't know, not sure," he says. "Depends on what's going on with my girlfriend."

"Wait a minute," I say, my heart dropping. "You have a girlfriend?"

"Yeah, I told you that last night," he says. "Right before you kissed me."

I'm quiet while I think about the events of the night, trying to recall if I ever heard the word girlfriend in the conversation. There was a whole lot of drinking and kissing and reading between glances, but I don't ever recall the mention of a girlfriend.

"You did not tell me that you had a girlfriend," I say, emphatically.

"Yes, I did," he says, just as confident.

"Alright," I say. "Well, I friended you on Facebook today so friend me back if you want to."

"Sure," he says. "I'll try to do that tomorrow."

"Tomorrow?" I ask. "Why tomorrow?"

"I just probably won't have time before then," he says.

"OK, well, I had a great time last night," I say. "It was great talking to you today too."

"Yeah, you too," he says. "Take care."

"You too," I say.

After we hang up two hours later, I sit up on my bed. I'm elated but irritated. Oh, that pisses me off. I knew it. I knew he was just way too good to be true.

CHAPTER EIGHT

The next day at work, I'm busy all morning with meetings, strolling from one to the next until it's time for lunch. When I finally get back to my desk, I have a Facebook friend confirmation from John. I'm excited, but apprehensive. I do not remember him telling me that he had a girlfriend. Dammit. Yes, it's just a girlfriend. No, it's not a wife. But either way, it's a relationship, and I don't want to be that girl. I've already been in that place, way back when I met my ex, the summer before my senior year of high school.

I login to my computer, then Jango, an internet radio program that allows users to make custom stations or just listen to genre stations like Hot Country or 80s Ballads or Techno. I stumbled upon it years ago when I was working on a system replacement project and needed music to help me crank out some major work output. The first song that flows out of the speakers brings tears to my eyes, Bryan Adam's 'Everything I Do, I Do It for You.'

Ironically, it's the homecoming song from 1991, when I was a candidate and the last thing I wanted was the lifelong label of being queen of anything. I had just met my ex that summer, but he had a girlfriend. We'd shared some kisses, but nothing more. I told him to come back when he figured out what he wanted. A few weeks later, he called me. He said he'd broken up with his girlfriend. He said he knew what he wanted.

I wish I would have known then that the way things started with us would have stayed with me the way that it did, always thinking that someday he would cheat on me. Now there are three kids to remind me that we had a good life together once. There are moments to remind me that life always seems so much better, so much simpler when you're looking back at it, like those were the days, that was the time. But when you're in it, it's something else. I suppose this is my own come back, my own karma, for the choice I made to be with him so many years ago, knowing that he had a girlfriend, but choosing to be with him anyway.

I spend the afternoon stalking John's profile on Facebook. I look at his status updates as far back as I can go. I look at his likes and his dislikes. I check out his friend list. I look at all of the pictures that I can see on his profile. If there's a girlfriend in the picture, he's doing a great job of hiding it. I already like him more than I should. There are pictures of him at home with his daughters, another of him at a wedding dancing with the bride, his sports car, a couple with his brothers and sisters and his mom, and a few from a recent football game. And my personal favorite, John on a 4-wheeler, wearing a simple green t-shirt and a pair of jeans. He's on chat so I open a new window to send him a message.

Hey there

Hello

Was just stalking your Facebook profile

Oh yeah

I love the picture of you on the 4-wheeler

You look hot

Thanks

Yeah

Where were you then

Out at my mom's house, Memorial Day weekend

Looks like you were having fun

Yeah, had beers and a bonfire later

That's cool, ttyl

I think back to what I was doing then, probably starting to emotionally unravel after discovering the truth that my ex had cheated on me. I skip back over to John's profile to see who our mutual friends are again. His younger brother and I became Facebook friends late last summer, followed closely by both of his sisters.

His oldest sister used to work with my brother at the local Coast-to-Coast hardware store, way back in the mid-80s. Once in a while, my mom would send me up there on my bike to get something for the house, batteries, light bulbs, duct tape. Usually my brother and John's sister would be standing at the counter laughing their asses off when I walked in the door. I'm pretty sure the phrase, 'Working hard or hardly working,' started from the antics that went on in that hardware store back then. After work, they would go road tripping, listen to music and pass around a bottle of booze to buzz them up a little harder.

His youngest sister was a year older than me in high school. We played sports together, sang in the choir, but we had different groups of friends. Based on her profile, it looks like she's married now, has a couple of dogs that she treats like kids, and lives about an hour north of here.

His brother was a couple of years older than me in high school, a 3-sport athlete, and a happy-go-lucky kind of guy. Of all the kids in John's family, he reminds me the most of his dad. He's once divorced and remarried, with two daughters, and rumor has it, he's got a little extra beer money in his pocketbook after he inherited some cash from an elderly neighbor who lived down the street from him. From what I can tell, he's probably John's best friend.

John mentioned on the phone last night that he was a big Minnesota Vikings fan, that he has season tickets, and that he is going to be at the Monday Night Football game when Brett Favre takes the field for the first time in purple and gold. I've been a Vikings fan all my life. Growing up, I remember Sundays were sacred, not only for church, but for watching the Vikes. My dad and my brother and I would watch the game while my mom brewed a pot of chicken noodle soup, or a beef roast mixed with peeled potatoes and carrots. Sometimes we even got to enjoy a fresh pumpkin pie with it, but mostly, by halftime, it was Schwan's ice cream. And usually it was my dad's favorite, good ol' Maple Nut.

When I was married, I would beg my husband to take us to a game, and once in a while, we would go. One year, I almost convinced him to buy season tickets. Now, I want to live a little, go to a football game as a single woman and see what kind of fun I can stir up. I want to find a way to go to that game, because somehow, someway, I figure I might be able to meet up with John once I'm there. I'm inspired by my plan. I log into my Stubhub account and start hunting down seats for the game. They have to be lower level, end zone or mid-field, under 100 bucks. There are 100s to choose from. Before I know it, it's 5 o'clock and I need to leave to get my kids. Before I pack up to go, I send an e-mail to Alicia and some of her friends to see if they are interested in going along to the game too.

Later that night, I get some e-mails back. A few of them are definitely interested, and a couple have invited some other friends too. The following day at work, I find seven lower-level end-zone tickets for seven ladies for the Monday Night Football game, where Brett Favre will be making history as he steps on the field for the first time donning the colors of his long-time rival. And I'm going to be there. This is gonna be good.

CHAPTER NINE

L ater that week, I start making plans for the first weekend without my kids since I moved into my new house. My youngest son has a Saturday morning football game, but after that, I'm wide open. I send a Facebook message to an old friend that I haven't seen in months.

Hey there

Hi, how are ya

Pretty good, just getting settled in my new house

Oh, that's awesome. Do you like it?

Yeah, I love it actually

5 bedrooms, 3 baths, so we have an office/guest room

It's right down the street from my parents

Good for you, I can't wait to come over and see it

Yeah, we'll have to find a time

Do you have any plans on Saturday?

We're having a Gopher football party

Wanna come over for it?

I might, that sounds like fun

I'm not a big college football fan, but if there's beer involved, I'm in

Of course there will be, and single guys too

Sounds perfect

What time, what should I bring

Whenever you can, no need to bring anything

I've got a football game in the morning, but then I'll be on my way

Sound good, see you then

In the car ride over to her house, I think about how Melanie and I met when we started working together back in 2000. I had just had my younger son, and she was pregnant with her first child. We formed a fast friendship grounded in our loves for beer and shopping. She loved me through the panic attacks that plagued me just after my daughter was born and when my family moved into the home in the country. On days when my anxiety was so high that I couldn't stand it anymore, we would get in the car and drive, sharing stories of our childhoods, secrets that haunted us, and dreams of escaping our everyday lives. Now she is a divorced puma of two and newly engaged to a younger man she met a couple of summers ago. I haven't met him yet, but she claims he's the love of her life.

When I get to her house an hour later, I hear voices suggesting that the party has already started. I ring the doorbell from the front porch of the 2-story house that she and her fiance' moved into together last summer. Quickly, Melanie's adorable blond pixie cut appears behind the glass door, dirty with fingerprints from her boys.

"Hey there," she says, her small bronzed frame pushing open the door for me to step inside.

"Hey, I brought some beer," I say, motioning to the case in my right hand.

"You didn't need to do that," she says.

"Well, I figure you probably wouldn't have enough beer for as much as I've been drinking these days, so I better bring my own," I tell her.

She laughs as the door slams behind me, then she wraps her arms around me for a hug.

"I've been thinking about you," she says.

"Well, thanks," I say. "It's been a really long summer. You look great."

"Well, you too," she says. "You've lost so much weight."

"Yeah, I lost quite a bit over the summer," I say, now 160 pounds on my 5'8" frame.

"Yeah, the game started a little while ago," she says. "We're just hanging out back here."

She turns around and starts walking through a room painted crimson red, centered by a high-top table with a chandelier hanging over it, and several cabinets housing antiques lining the walls.

"Oh, I love this room," I say, stopping to look around. "Where did you get that print?"

"Oh, at an auction in town," she says. "Isn't it fun?"

"Yes, I love it," I say, as she grabs my hand and leads me into the kitchen.

She walks over by a solid, handsome, strawberry-blond-haired man, with a baby face and a smile to match.

"Erika, this is Kyle," she says.

"Hey, Erika," he says, reaching out a hand to me. "I've heard a lot about you."

"Nothing but the good stuff, I hope," I say, smiling, realizing that he's probably heard it all, every juicy little detail.

She introduces me to his brother, mom, dad and stepmom, along with some other friends from work and high school. His brother is damn good-looking, but young, really damn young. It feels like the kind of party where you go to have a real good time but not necessarily meet a guy. Since I haven't been to her house before today, she offers to give me a quick tour.

"So, how are things going with mediation?" she asks.

"Good," I say. "We're already done. We spent about 3 hours in mediation a few days before school started and it was over. No alimony, no child support, just done. It feels good. I just want him to be a dad to our kids. That's all I really want."

She talks about her own divorce, the second one from the same man. She's a bit of history in the making, at least from my perspective. She is the only woman I know who has been married and divorced from the same man twice. But she's got two healthy, caring boys now, and she couldn't be happier, so I'm glad for that. She turns the conversation back to me.

"So, are you dating anyone yet?" she asks.

"No, just having some fun," I tell her, smiling, certain that she knows what I mean. "But I did hook up with someone last weekend and I can't stop thinking about him."

"Hmm," she says. "Sounds interesting. What's the story?"

"Well, I went to a wedding with my cousin, and I met this guy who grew up in town but then moved away," I say. "He probably used to work with your ex, actually."

"What's his name," she asks?

"I don't want to tell you," I admit.

"Why?" she asks.

"Well, apparently he has a girlfriend, and I don't want to be that girl, right?" I say.

"No, you definitely don't want to be that girl," she confirms. "But you can at least tell me his name."

"John Montgomery," I say, with a broken poker face.

"Oh, yeah, I've heard of him. I think he used to work with my ex, but I've never met him. What is this smile about?" she asks.

"I don't know," I tell her. "I like him. I spent one damn night with him, but I like him."

"Well, I can see that by the smile on your face," she says, smiling back.

"Melanie, we had sex three times in one night," I whisper as we're walking back downstairs.

She turns around, her dark brown eyes bulging, and says, "Are you kidding me?"

"No, I'm not. Once against the side of his car, another on the tailgate on our way home from the bar, and the last on my creaky damn bed with a roomful of people in the kitchen," I say. "I am definitely going to have to get rid of that bed!"

As we're walking back into the kitchen, the guys turn and look at us, like they want to know our secrets. I look at Melanie and hope she doesn't say anything. She turns to Kyle.

"So, do you know John Montgomery?" she asks.

Everyone else in the rooms stops talking and turns their head to look at us. I'm not really sure why she thinks that Kyle will know him, but now I'm definitely curious to hear the answer.

"Yeah, why?" he asks, turning to Melanie.

"Well, how would he know him?" I ask.

"Well, he probably works with him too," she says.

"So, why do you want to know if I know John or not?" Kyle asks.

"Oh, Erika met him last weekend," she says. "She was just wondering if you knew him."

"I was not wondering that!" I say. "You started it, lady."

"So, Kyle, do you know him?" she asks again.

"Yeah, he transferred a few years ago, but I see him every now and then at sales meetings," he says.

"So, what do you think of him?" she asks.

"Oh, John's a pretty good guy," he says. "He went through a bad divorce a few years ago and it sounds like he had a pretty tough time with it."

"Yeah," I say. "It was right around the time that his dad died, too."

"Yeah, and his ex was cheating on him too," Kyle's friend chimes in from the corner. "So how do you know John?"

"Well, I just met him last weekend," I say to the group that is now keenly interested in why we're talking about John Montgomery.

Damn, this is not going to be good. I dodge the rest of the questions, saying nothing at all, and then consider how I can change the subject, settling on the topic of football.

"So, how are those Gophers doing anyway?" I ask.

Melanie winks at me, recognizing my intentions, and the guys just start talking football again. Well, that was easy.

CHAPTER TEN

Two days later, I leave work early so that we can get up to the stadium, tailgate for a while, and maybe hunt down Mr. Montgomery. Before I leave, I head to the bathroom to throw on some jeans and my home Jared Allen jersey. I head over to Alicia's house to meet the rest of the ladies. I'm the last to get there, and they're waiting outside for me. I grab my overnight bag and throw it in the back of the car. A little after 3, we're on our way.

During the car ride, I touch up my makeup, then grab the purple pumps that I got over a lunch hour late last week and throw them on the floor of the car.

"Where in the hell did you get those shoes?" Alicia asks.

"Oh, after we booked the tickets to the game, I went to a few consignment stores to try to find some fun stuff to wear," I tell them.

"Those rock," she says.

"I know," I say. "And I got 'em for 17 bucks."

"No way," Alicia's friend says.

"And I got these cute earrings too," I say, grabbing them out of my purse and holding them up for everyone to see.

They're oohing and ahhing over them like ladies always do. Then we start talking about our plans for when we get to the stadium. About halfway there, it starts to rain, just lightly, which is going to make for an interesting evening if it keeps up. I'm not so worried about me because I have naturally curly hair that doesn't look too awful when it's wet, but some ladies can get a little high maintenance when their hair isn't just right. Hopefully we don't have any of that kind in our group. We stop at Catherine's apartment to leave the car there, then take the light rail downtown.

It's still raining when the light rail stops in front of the stadium, but a little harder now. And not one of us has an umbrella. When we get out of the car, there are people walking everywhere. I'd been to games before, but I'd never done any tailgating at the Dome. We follow the tracks and the movement of people. As we get closer to the stadium, the Black Eyed Peas "I Gotta Feeling" starts booming over our heads.

"Well, let's get a beer, ladies, should we?" I ask.

"Yes, please," one of Alicia's friends says.

At first, all we can find are beer stands with that horrible-tasting Miller Lite. But as we move farther into the crowd, and just before we're ready to settle for it, we crash into the Bloody Mary bar that also serves Michelob Golden Draft Light. It's not my favorite either, but it will do. I'm the first to get my beer, and as I'm waiting for the rest of the ladies to get a drink in their hand, I decide to send a text to John to let him know I'm at the game. I didn't say anything to him before, didn't tell him I was coming, in case it didn't work out for him to go, or if our plans fell through somehow.

Hey, are you at the stadium yet

Yeah, why

I'm here too

You're here, at the game?

Yeah, we're tailgating, just outside Gate B

We're inside the stadium already, section 110, stop over later if you want to

Hell yes, I will. We stand outside drinking our beer and socializing with the crowd until the light mist starts falling a little bit harder. Catherine has a sweatshirt that she throws over our heads like it's going to do any good at this point, and we all laugh at her gesture. I grab my camera out of my purse.

"Will you take our picture?" I say, approaching a guy in a twin Allen jersey just passing through.

"Yeah, sure," he says, sounding pissed off because he probably just wants to get in the stadium.

We pose together, drinks in the air and Catherine's sweatshirt barely covering us, while the cute single guy takes our picture.

"You two should take a picture with your matching jerseys," Alicia says, as he's handing the camera back to me.

"Sure," I say, handing my camera over to Alicia, then wrapping my right arm around the photographer.

"Smile," Alicia says.

"Thanks for taking our picture," I say, as he's walking away.

"Hmm," Alicia says. "You two were cute together."

"Really?" I ask. "You think so?"

"Did you get his name, or number, or anything?" Catherine asks.

"No," I say. "I didn't even think about it. Damn."

It's about an hour until game time, and the rest of the group wants to head into the stadium before it starts pouring. The lines are long, but the time goes fast with a buzz. While we wait, I send John another text.

We're on our way in now

Stop over when you get inside

The rest of the ladies want to grab a beer and head to our seats. I lean in a little closer to Alicia.

"I'm going to go over and say hello to John before the game, OK?" I tell her.

"OK?" she says, scowling. "Are you even going to sit in our seats at all?"

"Yeah, I am," I confirm. "I'll be over there after a little bit."

As I'm walking away, I already know that they're going to be mad at me. Alicia's scowl said it all, but I'm going to do it anyway. When I get to John's section and start making my way down the aisle just a few rows, I can see the back of his slightly balding head, making me smile. He's sitting at the end of the row by the aisle, three of his friends are lined down the row from him. I touch him on the back of his home Favre jersey, and he turns around, looking surprised to see me.

"Hey," he says, standing up. "You didn't tell me you were coming."

"Yeah," I say. "I just wanted to come over and say hello."

While he's standing, he introduces me to his friends, who are not really the most welcoming guys in the stadium. The friend seated next to him offers me his seat, and I take it as John moves over to sit closer to me. Now his friend has to stand in the aisle while we chat, but he's got a lot of nervous energy and he doesn't seem to mind. The beer man rolls through and the farthest friend from us stands up as he makes his way down the aisle.

"Anybody else want a beer?" he asks.

"I'm in," the other two say simultaneously.

"Yeah, sounds good," John says. "How about you? You want a beer?"

"Sure," I say, grabbing for my purse.

"No, I got it," the first one says.

"Are you sure?" I ask.

"Yep, I got it," he says again.

We all get a drink in our hand. I pull out my camera to get a picture of us, handing it to the friend standing in the aisle.

"Will you take our picture?" I ask.

He looks at John like he needs his permission first.

"Sure," he says, taking the camera from me.

We both set down our beers and I lean back into him while his friend takes the picture. Soon, the announcer asks the crowd to stand for the National Anthem. It's always been one of my favorite parts of a football game, a live band belting out The Star Spangled Banner. John and I both set down our beers and put our hands over our hearts. At the end of the anthem, I figure I should get back to my party with the ladies.

"Well, I'm going to head over to my seat now," I say, looking at John, as Guns and Roses 'Welcome to the Jungle' begins blaring throughout the stadium, signaling player introductions.

"Wait, what?" the nervous friend asks, still standing. "You're going to miss Favre's introduction, you know."

"True," I say. "I guess I can stay a little longer."

We're still standing as the crowd frenzy elevates waiting for Brett Favre's first introduction as a Minnesota Viking. All the years of being a Vikings fan and listening to the neighboring Packer fans brag about their quarterback was so worth the agony now, seeing him take the field in a purple jersey. When they announce his name, the crowd goes wild. Packer fans are hissing and booing, but they are outnumbered by the hometown crowd support for the new Minnesota hero.

"I have goose bumps," I say, turning to John, smiling.

"What?" he says.

"Goosebumps," I say, a little bit louder.

"Yeah," he hollers back, not wanting to carry on a conversation at an important time like this.

Shortly after kickoff, the friend who offered me his seat sits down next to me on the concrete steps.

"So, where are your seats?" he asks.

"We're over in the end zone," I say, pointing in the direction of our seats.

"I'll go over and sit in your seat and you can stay here, if you want," he offers.

"Are you sure?" I ask, not wanting to be a pain in the ass, but certain that I'd like to stay here with John.

I look at John. He shrugs his shoulders. I figure that if he didn't want me to stay, he would say so, or make it obvious. I don't want to interrupt his time with his friends, and I don't want to piss mine off any more than they already are.

"Yeah, that's cool," he says. "What's your seat number?"

"Hmm, 9 or 10," I say, pulling the ticket out of my jeans pocket, looking at it, then handing it to him. "10."

"Ok, I'll be back at the half," he says, grabbing it and then turning and bounding up the stairs.

I sit next to John for all of the first half, high-fiving with him and his friends. At one point, I wrap my arm around the backside of his seat until his friend on the end notices and shoots him a glance. Just before halftime, I catch him staring at the cheerleaders on the lower right corner of the field.

"What are you looking at?" I ask, smirking.

"Nothing," he says.

What a stupid answer. It immediately reminds me of my ex-husband. Something about a man and the answer 'nothing' just irritates me. I glance over in the same direction and watch the cheerleaders right along with him. Then I get a text from Alicia.

Are you coming over here or what

Yeah, I'll be over there at halftime

Well, you better hurry, you're missing all the fun

At the half, the Vikes are down by 7. John's friend comes back with a girl from our group. We stand and chat a minute, then John shoots me a look like it's probably time to give back his friend's seat. I stand and offer it back to him. Then, as I turn to follow her, she puts her hand behind her and I grab it as we head up the stairs. When we reach the top of the section, I turn back and am happily surprised when John is watching us.

"So, what's going on with you and John?" she asks.

"Nothing," I say. "Why?"

What I really want to say is 'none of your Goddamn business.'

"No reason," she says, shrugging her shoulders.

"I just met him when he was home last weekend," I tell her. "He asked me to come over and see him."

She doesn't say anything more as we hurry through the crowds and back to our seats. When we get there, the rest of the ladies aren't very happy with me.

"Where've you been?" Alicia asks.

"I was just sitting with John," I tell her.

"Well, you didn't tell me you were going to spend the whole first half over there," she says.

"I didn't really think that I was, but then his friend offered me his seat and said he would sit in mine," I say.

"Yeah, he was a peach," she says. "He was all over us, drunk and staggering."

"Oh, sorry," I say. "He wasn't really like that over by John."

"Where are his seats?" she asks.

"Over in 110," I tell her. "They're great seats."

She doesn't say anything. I can tell she's pissed off. I wave to the beer guy moving down the stairs.

"Anybody else want a beer?" I ask, turning to the rest of the ladies. "I'm buying."

They're all in. If they're anything like me, a free beer will forgive the minor offense of just wanting to sit at a football game with the guy who is making your heart race a little faster. Catherine hands her phone to some guys standing behind us that they befriended during the first half.

"Will you take our picture?" she asks, to the one who looks the most sober.

We get the group together for a pose, our hair all a mess from the rain, and drunk, all of us drunk on beer, friends and football.

The second half is completely different without John, or maybe it's just different because I'm watching a football game with a bunch of ladies who aren't as invested in the outcome as I am. In the end, the oldest quarterback in the NFL pulls the Vikes through to a 30-23 win over the Pack in a dramatic fourth quarter finish in the last couple minutes of the game. At the end of the game, while the rest of the group is deciding what to do next, I start texting with John.

Good ending, huh

Yeah, good game

Text me if you want to get together later

We're going out to the bars for a while

Probably home early

We're probably heading to some bars downtown, then to Catherine's

Text me later

As we head out of the stadium into the early October night, the air and wind feels good on my face, refreshing. We settle on Dan Kelly's bar, but after one drink, most of our group wants to head back to Catherine's apartment. I couldn't agree more and I send a text to John.

We're heading back now

John doesn't respond. By the time we get on the train and get to Catherine's house, it's 12:30. The rest of the group wants to go out. I'm awake but wasted. The only thing I'd rather be doing besides going to bed is going somewhere with John, or better yet, going to bed with him. I decide to call him and I'm startled when he answers.

"What are you doing?" he asks.

"Hey," I say.

"Hey," he throws back.

"What are you doing?" I ask.

"Just leaving a strip club," he says.

"What are you doing at a strip club when you could be somewhere naked with me?" I ask, teasing him.

"I don't know," he says. "Where are you?"

"I'm at Catherine's house in Eagan," I say. "We just got here."

"Well, I suppose you don't want to come back downtown then, huh?" he asks.

"Is that an invitation?" I ask.

"I guess so," he says, without confidence that I will.

"Why not? I can take a cab back," I say, having no idea how much time or money a cab is going to cost me at this time of night.

"Well, it's up to you," he says. "I'm heading to my hotel right now. I'll be there in 15 minutes."

"OK, well, when I get there I'm going to fuck you all night long," I say, confidently.

"Oh, really," he says. "Is that so?"

"Yes, it is," I yell into the phone. "I'm going to fuck the shit out of you."

"OK, bring it on," he says.

I feel like a horny, possessed woman who hasn't had sex in years. I have no idea what's come over me. Suddenly, Catherine's roommate scares the hell out of me when she appears from her bedroom.

"What's going on out here?" she asks.

"Nothing," I say, holding the phone away from my ear. "Sorry I woke you up."

"Well, some of us have to work tomorrow, you know?" she says, irritated with me.

"Sorry, I'm going to be leaving soon," I tell her.

With the smirk on my face, I'm sure that I do not appear the slightest bit sorry, but I don't know what else to say in the moment. I'm a little embarrassed that she overheard our conversation.

"Where are you going?" she asks me.

"I'm going to take a cab back downtown," I lie.

"Well, the girls are just down the road at a bar," she says. "They just texted me that they are coming home soon."

"I'll probably be gone before they get back," I tell her.

"Well, maybe you should wait," she says.

I'd like to tell her to go to hell, but I figure I'm in her apartment and that wouldn't be very nice. But I am a grown woman and if I want to go to meet a man in the middle of the night in downtown Minneapolis and make plans to fuck the shit out of him, then that's exactly what I'm going to do. Just as I think it, I realize how crazy it is, but I don't care. I'm going anyway. It would be crazy not to.

She turns around in a huff and heads back to her bedroom. I wonder if John just heard all that.

"So, are you coming or not?" he asks.

"Um, yeah," I say. "I'll be there in 15."

He tells me the name of the hotel that he's staying at, the streets that intersect, and to meet him in the lobby in 15 minutes. Next thing I know, I'm hopping in a cab and heading back into the bright lights of Minneapolis.

CHAPTER ELEVEN

When I get to the hotel, John is just arriving too. He looks as edible as a banana split in a Minnesota heat wave in the middle of the summer, nuts and whipped cream, everything. He's handsome as he steps out of the cab, still wearing his jersey and blue jeans. I follow closely behind him as he moves through the entrance, past the lobby and back to the elevators. When we get inside and the doors slowly close behind us, I move in closer to him, wanting to assault him so badly.

"Wait," he says, standing like a soldier, pokerfaced and solid. "Just wait until we get to the room."

It's strange, but I suppose his friends are probably staying at the same hotel and he probably doesn't want to collide with them when he has me along. I wait patiently because he asks me to, but as soon as the hotel room door closes behind us, I pounce all over him, pushing him up against the closet in the entryway, both hands pressed against his chest. I wish I wasn't so wasted right now, half-buzzed would be just about perfect for what I'd like to do with him. We turn in circles as we're kissing, and I move my body into him to force him toward the bed. When I push him, he falls over backward.

While he's lying there, I unbutton his jeans and tug at his zipper. I can't get it with one hand. I think it's because his junk is just too damn big to make it over the hump. When I finally get it, I pull his jeans down over his knees, but I can't wait any longer to get at his rock hard cock. I put my mouth down over him, taking all of him in. Up and down, over and over. He's moaning, then he grabs the sides of my face and pulls me farther over him. I feel like I could do this all night long. As drunk as he is, he probably thinks so too. I have no idea how much time has passed until his hands slowly fall off to the sides at his waist. I look up at him, ready to fuck. And there he is, fast asleep and snoring. It reminds me of a book that my daughter and I sometimes loan out from the local library about a bed full of sleepy bears, who one by one roll over and 'fall faaast asleep' in their soft feather bed while their mama reads them a bedtime story. I guess that was my bedtime story for him tonight.

"John, are you really sleeping?" I say. "John?"

I laugh out loud, secretly hoping it will startle him awake so we can finish, but he's out. I just watch him for a little while, his face looking innocent when he's sleeping. I take off my jeans and pull the covers out from underneath him. In my football jersey and purple panties, I crawl in next to him, snuggling in under his arm. Tomorrow, there will have to be paybacks for him falling asleep on me, but tonight, I'm right where I want to be.

The next morning, John is up before me. I hear him go to the bathroom, but I have no idea what time it is because I can't find my phone. Then I look up at the alarm clock. It's 7:30. Cripes, by the time we met at the hotel and finally went to bed it was probably 2 a.m. When he comes back to bed, I roll over toward him. He moves his hand across my body and lays it on my ass. We lie there for a few minutes before I get up to go to the bathroom.

When I get in the bathroom, I have blood all over my panties. Dammit, that sucks. I thought I had one more day before I got my period. Now this whole damn trip is wasted. I don't even have a tampon with me. When I get back to bed, John's cock is hard and ready to go. I'd had sex plenty of times when I was married and had my period, but I didn't know if I was ready for this with someone I just met. He rolls over and pulls my jersey up over my hips.

"We've got a little problem," I say, coyly.

"What?" he asks.

"I don't really know how to say it to you," I tell him. All of a sudden, I feel like a teenage girl having sex for the first time.

"What?" he asks. "What is it?"

"I got my period," I tell him.

"So what," he says, shrugging his shoulders.

I trust him. And it just feels comfortable. I roll on top of him and slip his penis inside me. We get into a rhythm for a little while, but then I slow down.

"What's wrong?" he asks.

"Nothing," I say, lying.

This just doesn't feel right. I've had plenty of sex toward the end of my period but not on the first day. On white sheets, no less. I swing my body around so he can come at me from behind. He stands up and moves around me, then eases into me. I am so wet. I don't even want to look at what a mess it is. It never bothered me when I was married. I don't know why it does now. Across the room, I'm watching him banging into me in the mirror attached to the dresser, and it turns me on. Then he turns his head and he's looking at me too.

He pulls out and goes to the bathroom to clean himself up. I lie down on the bed and wait for him. When he comes back, he lies down next to me and draws me in closer, spooning me for a few minutes. And as quickly as he laid down, he gets back up and looks at his watch. Suddenly, he is in a hurry. I get up and go to the coffee pot to make some coffee.

"Are you leaving soon?" I ask.

"Yeah, we've got a long drive today," he says, looking at his phone.

I find my phone to text Alicia.

"I'll have to see if Alicia will come here and get me," I say.

"I can give you a ride if you want," he offers.

"No, that's OK. I can take the train," I tell him.

He watches me while I'm texting Alicia, the coffee still brewing.

Hey, are you up

Yeah, what's up

Can someone come get me

Why don't you just take the train

Which stop is it

#13, text when you get to the station and we'll pick you up

OK, ttyl

John has the TV on now and is sitting on the end of the bed watching the highlights from the game last night. I move closer and stand beside him few minutes.

"Well, I'm going to head out," I tell him. "They're going to pick me up at the station when I get there."

"Are you sure you don't want me to give you a ride?" he asks.

"Nope, I'm good. I know you want to get going," I say.

I go back to the coffee pot and pour myself a cup. Then I pour one for John and hand it to him.

"Thanks," he says, looking surprised, like I'm a grown up for making coffee and actually sharing it with him.

"You're welcome," I say.

We stand there for a moment, both sipping our coffee. Then, out of nowhere, he shocks the hell out of me.

"So, would you ever consider getting together with Lauren?" he asks, obviously amused at the idea.

Lauren is a young woman we both know, a beautiful girl, smart, with a glowing personality. But young, goodness is she ever young.

"You mean, like a threesome?" I ask. "You and me and her?"

"Yeah, something like that," he says, not wanting to be too invested in the idea if I were to say no.

"Yeah, probably not," I say politely. "She's awfully young. And I know her family."

Not that I've never considered the idea, but Lauren is just not the right girl in the scenario for me.

"Well, I better get going," I tell him.

I step closer to him. He grabs the sides of my face, pulls me in and then, instead of kissing my lips, he raises his head up and kisses me gently on the forehead. It makes me feel young, endearing. In fact, I don't think I've ever had anyone else kiss me on my forehead in my life, not even my dad. I turn and open the door without saying goodbye, looking back waving and smiling as he watches me. Then I'm gone.

When I get to the lobby of the hotel, I have no idea where I'm going. As I step outside, it's cold and all I'm wearing is my jersey from the night before. I'm already shivering. I have jeans and my purple high heels on. My feet are freezing, like purple icicles are hanging out from the bottom of my pants. I hail a taxi and ask the driver how to get to the closest light rail station. The scowl on his face suggests he's irritated with me for stopping him for directions, but he gives them to me anyway. I have to walk three blocks in the winter without a jacket. I guess it's what I get for leaving the ladies last night and going for my romp with John.

On the walk to the station, it starts to spit rain, not hard, but the kind that's going to continue all day long. When I get to the station, the train is just leaving and I'm drenched all over. I wait 15 minutes for the next one to roll through, wondering why I didn't just take John up on his offer to drive me. I already know the answer. Because I don't want to be a pain in the ass.

After the train arrives at the station near Catherine's apartment, I text Alicia to let her know that I'm there. I figure it's been over an hour so by now they should be up and ready to go.

Hey, I'm at the station

It's going to be a little while

Why

Everyone is still sleeping

Well, I thought you wanted to get going

We do, we're getting up

OK, well I'll just be here waiting

I hang out at the station for 20 minutes, watching people and trains come and go, before I text her again.

How long's it going to be?

They just got up

OK, well I'm standing here in the rain

Yeah, I know, we're trying to hurry

OK, see you in a bit

Another 15 minutes goes by and I don't hear anything back from Alicia. I've probably watched 20 trains come and go by now. I'd like to get back on one and head back into downtown and snuggle with John in his hotel room all day.

Where are you guys?

We're just getting in the car, be there in 10

OK, see you in a bit

Another 10 minutes later, as I'm shivering and shaking from the cold, they finally pull up in Alicia's car. They park across the lot and make me walk over to meet them.

"What the hell took you guys so long?" I ask.

"I told you, we were waiting for Holly to get ready," Alicia says.

I turn to her in the front seat.

"Well, that was nice of you to make me wait over an hour for you," I say.

"Whatever," she says, furiously. "You took off last night and we didn't even know where you went."

"I told Alicia I was going to meet John downtown," I shoot back.

"No, you just told me you were going back downtown, but you didn't say why," Alicia shouted.

"Well, fuck you," I shout to all of them. "I wouldn't make you wait an hour before I came to pick you up, especially when it was right down the road and it's raining outside."

"Well, you shouldn't have left last night then, I guess," she says.

"Whatever," I say. "Fuck you."

I know damn well that she would do the same damn thing to get a piece of ass as fine as his. Whatever.

The rest of the car ride is pretty damn peaceful. I'm sure they are all giving me the silent treatment, but it's the biggest backfire ever. With the way that my head is throbbing, I'm enjoying it. When we get back to Alicia's house, I drive straight home to take a nap. A few hours later, I get up, check my e-mail and send a text to John.

Are you on your way home?

Not yet

I thought you were heading home right away

We're going to the Twins game tonight

Well, thanks for inviting me ;)

Got the tickets from work

Nice. Have fun.

Silently followed by 'you son-of-a-bitch.' I can't believe he didn't say anything about going to the Twins game. I love the Twins. It's the end of the season and it's the middle of the playoffs. When I get home that afternoon, I immediately hop on Facebook to check out John's profile to see if he posted anything about the game, but there is nothing.

Some of the ladies have already added their photos and tagged me, so I head out to the kitchen to grab my camera to upload mine. I dig through my purse, twice. I go back to my bedroom and tear through the clothes on my bed. Nothing. I head out to the garage to check my car, thinking it might have fallen out of my purse on the way home. Nothing. I can't find it anywhere. I shoot a text to Alicia.

Hey, did you guys find my camera

No, why

I lost it

You could check with Catherine to see if you left it there

OK, can you send me her number

When I get the number, I immediately send a text to her.

Hey there lady, it's Erika

Hey

You didn't happen to find a camera around your place did you

Umm, no

Well, it's mine if you do

OK, I'll let you know

The last time I remember having it in my hands was when I dug my phone out of my purse in the morning, and I set it down on the dresser where the TV was sitting. I send a text to John.

> Hey, you didn't happen to find my camera in the hotel room did you

> No why

> I can't find it

> If you did, I'm sure it's already gone

> OK, thanks anyway

Well, after the car ride home, I wouldn't be surprised if one of them tossed it out the window or something. I guess John and I will have to do it all again sometime. And hopefully, it will be real damn soon.

CHAPTER TWELVE

The week after the game goes by fast. My kids are back home with me and the nights are filled with homework, Girl Scouts, open gym, and dinners alone with them. At work, I'm just getting started on a new project to solicit contracts for a new product to collect payments for different kinds of services. I conduct a couple of interviews with some stakeholders, do some online research of typical product features, then put together a draft of requirements document to share with the rest of the team.

The following Saturday, the kids and I are just hanging out together, watching TV, playing Xbox, checking Facebook. After lunch, I login to check my newsfeed and somebody has posted a 'Like' for a song I've never heard before, "Two is Better Than One," by Boys Like Girls. I click on the link to hear the song.

So maybe it's true, that I can't live without you

Well maybe two is better than one

There's so much time, to figure out the rest of my life

And you've already got me coming undone

I'm thinking, two is better than one

Becca and I listen to it a few more times. It's a little cheesy for me, a little school-girlish, but I have to admit that I like it. It makes me feel like a young girl, the fairytale, the love story. Two people together, a man and a woman. Two parents, a mother and a father. After thinking about it a little longer, it makes me angry. Dammit, I wanted that for my life, for my kids, and then my ex had to go and fuck it all up. But hey, maybe next time will be different. Maybe I'll actually find someone who wants to be in a committed relationship, be faithful, be a family man.

"Mommy," she says. "Who's that guy?"

She points at the screen, dirtying it up with her chubby little pointer finger. It's a picture of John wearing a black shirt that very nicely accents his peppered hair.

"Oh, he's someone that I met a few weeks ago," I say, my face brightening.

"When?" she asks.

"Remember when I told you about that wedding I was going to with Alicia?" I ask.

"Yeah," she says.

"Well, I met him then," I say. "We went for a ride in his car, and then he came back here for pizza and a beer."

"Ohh," she says, her voice rising and falling and her eyes widening.

Then, she doesn't say anything. Thinking about her mom being with another man is going to take some time to digest. That's probably going to be just enough information for a little while, so I leave it alone.

In the afternoon, I decide to mow the lawn while my kids are busy playing in the neighborhood. I love mowing, even now as a grown woman. I love to just breathe in the fresh air, see the rows in the lawn when it's finished, one after the other, so neat and tidy.

When I was a teenager, I would mow the lawn for my dad because he worked 12-hour days, mostly in manufacturing facilities. My parents worked different shifts for the longest time, my dad worked nights and my mom worked days. The summer before 7th grade, my dad took off for Alaska to work on a fishing boat, trying to earn enough money to put himself through tech school for the next year without having to work. That's the summer I learned how to mow the lawn, starting the mower and putting in the gas. My brother was already 16 with a car and a job and a girlfriend. But me, I was home free, lounging at the pool, making frosting and melted cheese for lunch, and mowing the lawn to help my mom out. Some days, when it was hotter than a whore in church, I hated it. But mostly, I loved it.

When I get outside to start the mower today, it's a high sun, crisp air kind of day. I realize I don't have enough gas in the tank to finish the job. I holler across the yards to let the kids know I am heading to the gas station. On the way there, I crank up the radio, flipping through the stations until I land on the end of Tesla's "Love Song," which rolls right into "Broken Wings." Of course, I think of John and I grab my phone to text him.

Hey, whatcha up to

When I get to the station and just start pumping the gas, my phone rings with a text back from him.

Just mowing the lawn

Crazy, me too, push or rider

Rider, why

I'd love to hop on and go for a ride ;)

Sounds like fun to me

Be careful, texting while driving is dangerous

Ha, funny

Wait a minute, I guess riding him while mowing would be a little dangerous too. When I get back home, I mow the lawn, thinking of John, with a huge happy smirk on my face all the while.

❖

That evening, when my kids and I sit down to a dinner of homemade spaghetti and meatballs, I decide that I need to give my kids a pep talk for what's about to transpire with our family life.

"So, you guys know that your dad and I finished mediation a couple of weeks ago, right?" I ask.

My oldest looks up from his plate, spaghetti spilling out of his mouth, like he's going to vomit if he has to hear the word divorce even one more time.

"Your dad is going to live in the house in the country, but he says that he might move closer to work after a while," I say.

"Why, mom?" Bennett asks.

"I don't know why, Bennett," I say, lying. "But I'm going to live here in town, regardless of what your dad does, so that you guys can keep going to the same schools and be here with your friends, alright?"

"Well, Janet and the girls already stayed at dad's house last weekend," Bennett says.

Janet is my old best friend. Bryce stops eating and stares at Bennett, hoping it will shut him up.

"We had a big sleepover in the basement, and dad and Janet slept in your bedroom," Bennett says, his tattling voice coming on now.

"Yeah, the girls and I got to sleep on the air mattress together," Becca says, smiling.

"Well, that's lovely," I say. "I'm glad they're not wasting any time."

Bryce stares at me now, his eyes begging me to not go any further.

"Mommy," my daughter says, just her voice making my tears start.

"What, sweetie?" I ask, my throat cracking.

"Do you think you and Janet will ever be friends again?" she asks.

The boys' heads both shoot up from being buried back in their spaghetti. I suppose she's wondering what any 6-year-old would, since she's seen Janet and me in our better days, hanging out by our pool, going for pedicures together with our girls, shopping every once in a while on a weekend. You know, best friend kind of stuff. Oh, and fucking my husband.

"Well, Becca, right now, I would have to stay no." I say, trying to be sensible, not wanting to lose my temper or cry. "I don't really consider Janet a friend of mine anymore, and I don't really see how that would change. She hasn't been a very good friend to me at all."

Bryce looks sternly at me and I know he's angry for what I just said. He likes Janet very much, for all the right reasons, mostly because he's known her for most of his life. He throws his fork on top of his plate.

"I'm done," he says, picking up his place and stomping over to the sink.

Yeah, me too.

On Sunday morning, I go to wake the kids from their beds around 7:30 for church. I haven't been to church in a long, long time. And today it's more for myself than it is for them. My ex would never go to church with me, and he never understood why I wouldn't just go alone. Now, I I'll have to go alone anyway, so that's just what I'm going to do.

I head downstairs to get the boys in the shower. My youngest son is watching TV. He's always been a morning guy, up and at it while the rest of us sleep.

"Alright, kiddo, time to get in the shower," I say.

I know this church thing is going to shock the hell out of all three of them, but I figure he'll be the easiest.

"Why?" he asks. "I thought we didn't have anything going on today."

"Nothing besides church," I say.

"What?" he says, throwing the remote down on the ground. "You never told me we had to go to church today."

"Yeah, well, we're going," I say. "So get up, get in the shower, and get your shit done. And let your brother know when you're done."

As I turn around to head back upstairs, he mumbles something under his breath, and I don't even want to know what it is. This single mom stuff is going to be a helluva good time.

When we get to church, we're a few minutes late and the kids want to sit in the balcony. I decide to give in to their request, hoping that it means they'll behave. By the time we get settled in our seats, it's already time for the first reading. It's from the book of Mark, with a practical reminder about the rules around divorce in the church.

"Whoever divorces his wife and marries another commits adultery against her, and if she divorces her husband and marries another, she commits adultery," the lector says.

I want to send a laugh loud and clear over the railing directly in front of me, directly out over the congregation. I wonder about the husband who is fucking his wife's best friend. Maybe there is a special verse just for guys like that. I'll have to get back to my bible verses I guess. It just sounds like a bunch of garbage to me. Right now, if a man leaves his wife and marries another, he's probably crazy anyway, because after what I've been through in my first marriage, I don't know why anybody would get married twice.

CHAPTER THIRTEEN

Late Sunday afternoon, my kids leave to go to their dad's house and I'm on my own again, left to fill the time and space that comes with joint custody. During a lunch hour one day at work. I jump on the Vikings' web site to figure out when I might be able to go to another game. I discover that they are headed to Green Bay to take on the Packers in a few weeks. All my life I've wanted to go to Lambeau Field for a football game. I figure if I can find some friends who don't mind paying the price of the tickets, it will be a great trip for a bunch of women. I send out a message to some ladies to see if they are interested. I hear back from a couple, but by the time I check out ticket prices, lower-level seats are already at $275. Luckily my friend Sara messages me back and tells me she's in. By late afternoon, I've got two tickets to the Vikes/Pack game, and a free night hotel with some points I have on a credit card. And even better, Sara volunteers to drive.

Later that afternoon, I login to Facebook to update my status.

Heading to Lambeau for the Vikes/Pack game in a few weeks!

I get a few 'Likes' and some comments, then a chat from my old friend Brad.

Heading out to Green Bay, huh?

Yeah, Sara and I are going

That should be fun

Oh yeah, I've always wanted to go to a game there

Me too, lucky

Don't be hooking up with any Packer fans when you're there

I'll try to stay out of trouble ;)

Ttyl

The night before the trip to Lambeau is Halloween. For the first time in 13 years, I'll be celebrating without my kids. It's a little bittersweet for me. I only have a couple of years left before they won't even dress up at all. I decide to dress up like something that I would never be in real life: a naughty nurse. The fact that I faint at the sight of blood and that I've never really been much of a naughty anything should make for a pretty good showing.

My costume is hilarious, sexy, over the top. I borrowed it from Alicia, who is short and petite, nothing like me. It's a white vinyl mini-dress with red vinyl accents on the sleeves, on the border of the skirt and all the way down the full-length zipper down the front. It barely covers my ass. I put on a pair of black vinyl over-the-knee boots, white tights and a triangle-shaped hat made of white vinyl with red accents. I top it off with fake eyelashes, a stethoscope, garter belt and a syringe. Just as I'm about to walk out of the house, I throw my phone over my head to take a picture, getting a very good shot of my cleavage. I pull it up, ok it for distribution, and text it to John.

It's packed when I walk into Snowball's, people in the upper bar and even more in the back room dancing to the band. I'm barely able to make it through the crowd to the banquet hall where the band is playing. I see Alicia across the room in her race car driver attire. We head to the bar to get a beer together.

As we're chatting about the crowd of costumes, I can feel someone staring at me across the room. It feels like the first night I met John. I keep looking, keep scanning the room. I can feel them on me, but I just can't find them. Finally, my eyes lock with somebody wearing an old man's costume. The mask is creepy though, with wrinkles and scars, a long nose dotted with moles, and the person is wearing a flannel shirt and bib overalls. The body is taller than me, definitely over 6 feet tall and there is another person wearing a similar costume, but the mask is an elderly woman. All I can see through the mask are the person's eyes, and we're locked together, like a couple of dogs in heat that can't be separated.

As I'm walking away from the bar to approach the mysterious eyes, the owner of the bar grabs me.

"Hey lady," he says, tugging at my arm. "You want to take a picture with me?"

"Well, sure. Get over here," I say, pulling him into me and wrapping my leg around him, half my ass probably hanging out the back of my dress.

One of the bartenders comes around from behind the bar to get the shot. I follow him on his way back to the bar. After I get my beer, I start heading in the direction of the couple, but as I get closer to where they were standing, they are already gone. The rest of the people in their group are still standing there, dancing and drinking and hanging out.

Alicia comes over and grabs me to dance, and then we take a couple of shots like it's just what the doctor ordered. Before I know it, it's 2 a.m. and I have to get up in the morning. I beg her to take me home. It's 3 before I get there, and in three hours, I have to get up to get ready to leave for the game. I'm pretty sure I'm still going to be drunk when Sara shows up to pick me up at 7 a.m.

Sure enough, three hours of sleep is not enough time to sleep off the shots we thought we needed at the end of the night. I hit my alarm twice. Finally at 6:30, I get out of bed. I'm thankful that Sara's driving, because otherwise I'd probably get a DUI. She's right on time at 7, but I don't roll out of the house until 7:15. She's laughing at me as I approach the car. Shit, I either look like hell or still drunk, or maybe both. It's going to be a long drive.

"Good morning," she says, grinning. "How are you feeling this morning?"

"Well, I'm still drunk, and I only got three hours of sleep last night," I tell her. "So it could be a long day."

She just looks at me and laughs.

"You'll be fine," she says, trying to reassure me. "You don't look too bad for only having three hours of sleep."

"Well, thanks," I say. "But I feel like hell."

"You can sleep along the way," she tells me.

"No way," I say. "I'm not going to sleep. I don't want to miss anything. I'll just wake up cranky anyway."

We get my bags settled and I hop in the front seat. As she's backing out of my driveway, she asks how we get there.

"How should I know?" I ask her. "You're driving!"

"I know, but I figured you would know," she says, sounding concerned.

"Oh, we'll be fine. Take the back roads to the interstate and we'll take it all the way there," I tell her.

We head out of town. She starts asking about my night out, the costumes, what I wore. Then we talk about my kids and how they're handling the divorce, how I'm doing, her own divorce so many years ago. We're already halfway into our 4-hour drive when Sara asks if I want to stop for something to eat. She's got to put gas in the car too. When we get back in the car, we're both quiet for a while. I get out my phone and decide to send a text to John.

Good morning sunshine!

Heading to Green Bay for the game tonight

Then I tell her the story of me and John. I'm sure it's written all over my face how I feel about him.

"I haven't seen him in years," she says. "He used to be so handsome. Is he still as hot as he used to be?"

"Hell yeah," I tell her, smiling.

About 10 minutes later, as we're turning to head north toward Green Bay, we drive through a little town that probably has more cows than people. Apparently, it's the Dairy Capital of the World or some damn thing. And right in the middle of the town is an enormous 3D-version of a Holstein cow, bigger than a truck.

"Stop the car," I tell Sara.

"What? Why?" she asks.

"We gotta getta a picture with that animal," I say.

She laughs and says, "You've got to be kidding me?"

"No, I'm not. Have you ever seen a damn cow in the middle of a town like that?" I ask her.

"Well, no," she says. "I guess I really haven't."

Clearly, she thinks I've lost my mind.

"Well, get over here," I say. "We need a picture of this."

I ask a passerby to take the picture. By the look on his face, he thinks I'm crazy, but he probably passes through here all the time. He takes a picture anyway. We thank him and hop back in the car. Now we're less than 30 minutes from Green Bay. We decide to head to our hotel before we go to the stadium. When we get there, the front desk clerk tells us that they have a shuttle that will take us to the stadium, and he asks if we're interested. He says there are a couple of guys that are leaving in about 20 minutes and we can join them and split the cost. Sara and I look at each other.

"Sounds great," we say in unison.

We head to our room, use the bathroom and throw on our jerseys. Minutes later, we're in the backseat of a mini-van headed to Lambeau Field, living the Midwest America dream.

We chit chat with the shuttle driver and the other 2 guys on the way there, but when we turn on the street that takes us to the stadium, Sara and I are both suddenly quiet.

"Oh, my, gosh," I say, finally.

"Wow, it's huge," Sara says. "I can't believe how different it looks in person."

"Wow," I say.

The driver drops us at the very front of the building and we throw some money together and hand it to the driver. We part ways with the two guys and slowly ease our way into the sea of green and gold.

"I can't believe I'm actually here," I say, to anyone who can hear me. "This trip has been on my bucket list for as long as I can remember."

"Yeah, me too," she says. "Unbelievable."

I stand back and just take the whole place in. The Vikes taking on the Packers at Lambeau Field, and Brett Favre is going to be wearing purple. The whole moment inspires me.

"How about another picture?" I ask her.

"Sure," she says, rolling her eyes.

"Well, jeez," I say. "We're making history today, you know. I've never been to an away game."

"Me neither," she says.

We hunt down another guy to take our picture, and then we head toward the line to get into the stadium. After 15 minutes of being plagued by mostly green and gold, we get felt up by a cute, Black security officer who asks if we want to stick around and keep him company.

"No," I shout as we head inside. "We've got to find a beer stand."

I check our tickets for our section number.

When we get inside, the first thing we do is head for a beer stand.

"Where are our seats?" Sara asks.

"We're in 103," I tell her.

Over our head, there's a sign pointing us toward our section, and minutes later, we're already there. Then our beers are gone. I look at the clock on my phone.

"We've got 45 minutes before the game starts," I say. "Wanna get another beer and take a walk around the stadium?"

"Sure," Sara says.

As we head out of the stadium, we get stares from Packers fans everywhere. I want to flip them off but decide we probably don't want to get in a fight in a city where we literally know no one. When we get to the beer stand, I heckle the clerk.

"What are you lookin' at?" I ask, sarcastically.

I feel like we might as well be a couple of hookers standing on a street corner or something the way he is staring at us.

"Nothing," he says. "Just checking out a couple of good lookin' women, that's all."

"Aww, well, that's nice," Sara says, smiling.

I smile too. I feel like we should be sucking up to him instead of the other way around, so maybe we could get some free beer or something. We stand and chat a few minutes. He asks where we're from and he tells us the same. He tells us to stop back again, and then we're off walking around the stadium. We're checking out guys, and they're checking us out. Sara is married but it's no crime to look. I tell her what I like in a guy and she starts pointing some out as we walk.

"How 'bout him?" she asks, gesturing at a taller guy, dark, curly hair, with a freakin' Packers jersey on.

"Wrong team," I tell her. "My brother warned me before I left not to hook up with any Packer fans while I was here, and definitely don't bring any back home."

Sara laughs.

"No, seriously, he really told me that," I say.

We pass a clock. Ten minutes to game time.

"We better get heading back to our seats," I tell her.

"Oh jeez, you're right. Our section is this way," she points back in the direction we just came from.

The corridor is clearing out now, so we can walk faster. By the time we get to our seats, we miss the kickoff. And then, when I look up at where our seats are supposed to be, there are people sitting there already.

"What the hell is going on?" I ask.

"I don't know," Sara says. "Where are the tickets?"

I pull them out from my purse and we both look at them.

"This says Section 113," Sara says, looking up at the signs around the stadium. "113 is that way."

"Shit," I say. "How in the hell did I mess that up?"

Sara just looks at me, shaking her head. We turn around and head down the stairs to double-time it over to our seats. And of course, we grab a beer on the way.

Our seats are perfect. In fact, I doubt that there's a bad seat in the whole place. The only thing that could have made it the least bit better is if we didn't have to sit in the middle of a bunch of pissed-off Packer fans when we beat their asses. They are whining, throwing shit and just plain rude as we walk out of the stadium. Bunch of freaking babies.

CHAPTER FOURTEEN

After the game, we head across the street to a bar where the locals hang out. The place is packed and it takes us 20 minutes to get our first beer. That's probably alright because we were pretty drunk when we left the game anyway. We take a walk around the place. There are 3 different rooms that are part of the bar. In the farthest room from the door, there are about 15 tables with a bunch of guys standing around playing pool. There is a smaller bar on the opposite end of the tables. In the middle room, there are a bunch of smaller high-top tables, all full of people. We head back toward the first room, which has a huge rectangular bar and a jukebox blaring. There are also a few pool tables on one side of the bar.

A couple of seats open up at one end of the bar and Sara heads over to try to snatch them up. I've never seen anything like it; the bar is like an 80/20 ratio of men to women. It still takes us 10 minutes to get a bartender's attention, and ironically, it's a woman. After we get our drinks, we just sit and check out the rest of the bar. On the opposite side of us, there is a tall, younger looking guy wearing a Minnesota Gophers jersey. He's handsome, but I can't get a look at his hands so I tell Sara I'm going to get a little closer. As soon as I get within 3 feet of him, I see his ring. I want to turn around and head back to my place at the bar but then one of the other older guys in his group sees me watching him.

"Hey there, pretty lady," he says, trying to let me down easy. He's balding, with a moustache, a little heavier.

Damn, this single lady stuff isn't as fun as I thought it was going to be.

"Well, hey there," I say, blushing. "How 'bout that game?"

Another guy in the group chimes in, saying, "Yeah, I've been to a lot of games here, but this was definitely the best."

"This is my first time," I say. "I was a Lambeau Field virgin until today."

They all laugh. The handsome guy just smiles at me, probably knowing I was on my way over there after him.

"This is my son-in-law," the first guy says, putting his arm around him like he's marking his territory. I feel like if I was alone in a room with the guy we probably wouldn't be able to keep our hands off each other. But right now, his father-in-law is all over me.

"Nice to meet you," I say, holding out my hand to shake his. I still don't know his name, but I guess I don't really need to.

"We're here for his bachelor party," the father-in-law explains.

"Wow, lucky guy," I say. "So you've got just a few nights of freedom left, I guess, huh?"

"Yep," the father-in-law says. "He's marrying my beautiful daughter next weekend."

"Well, good luck to you," I say, winking. "You guys have a fun night."

As I turn to walk back to our spot at the bar after striking out, I hear roars of laughter behind me. Damn, I didn't really think I was that funny. Across the bar, I see Sara standing talking to a couple of new guys that joined her.

"Hey, Erika. While you were off flirting across the bar, these guys just bellied up to the bar next to us. This is Joe," she says, motioning to the guy on the left, sitting closer to her. "And this is Steve, and Steve's sister."

His sister pipes in, "I don't want to be 'Steve's sister,'" she says. "I've got a name, you know," looking at Joe.

"Nice to meet you," I tell them, laughing. "Where are you guys from?"

They explain that they are originally from the area, but they both live in California now and work in Hollywood. I'm sure they are lying, but I go along with it anyway.

"Hmm, sounds like fun work," I say, trying to get the waitress' attention. The male bartender is gone now. I feel like I'll probably die thirsty in this bar in Green Bay, surrounded by Packer fans, and no one will help me because we beat them in overtime. Suddenly, the guy comes around from the other side of the bar. I tipped him well last time so he heads right over to me. Sara and I order a beer.

"I got it," Steve says. He turns to Joe and asks if he wants something.

"You don't have to do that," I tell him.

I look at his hands, no rings. He's a good looking man, dark, a little bit longer hair, deep green eyes, very tan for November. The only problem is that he's got a Packer shirt on. I have to give him shit.

"Well, thanks for the drink, but my brother warned me to not hook up with any Packer fans while I was here," I tell him.

Steve looks at Joe.

"Well, Steve's married anyway," he says. "But I'm not."

Oh, sure. Isn't that just how it always goes. The hot guy is married and the creepy one is into me.

"So, would you consider taking a picture in my Packer t-shirt?" he asks.

"What do you mean, like put it on?" I ask.

"Yeah, and get a picture with me?" he asks.

Wow, I've got to think about that one for a minute. If my brother gets wind of the picture, I'm never going to live it down. In fact, he'll probably disown me, or at least change me as the beneficiary on his life insurance policy. Big decision.

"Yeah, I guess I can do that," I say, winking.

He grabs the bottom of his shirt and starts pulling it up over his head. Everyone around the bar seems to turn to stare, like he's a porn star just getting started in his first scene, except that he's creepy. After he gets it off, he hands it to me. I grab it and throw it over my head, tousle my hair and wrap my arm around him as Sara grabs my camera for a picture.

"Smile," she says. "C'mon, you two. Smile!"

I feel like I already am, but I turn it up a notch.

"Good," she says, giving us the thumbs up.

Suddenly, her phone starts vibrating on the top of the bar and she picks it up.

"Oh, I'm going to go outside a minute," she says. "Some old friends of mine are outside, on their way out of town."

While she's gone, I stand and chat with them about my job and kids. It's almost 1 a.m. when Sara comes back in the bar and I'm watching a couple making out in a corner booth, tongues lashing, his hands up her shirt, hers down his pants. She's a Packer and he's a Viking. We're both staring in disbelief when Sara tells me she's getting tired, that she's ready to go.

We're just saying our goodbyes to our new friends when across the room, a younger guy walks through the side door into the bar. He's taller, light brown hair, good looking and no ring. He's got a hunting hat on, one of those weird ones with the flaps down over his ears. It reminds me of college where a lot of guys at my alma mater wore stuff like that. The only 'infidelity' in my life was a little smooching with a guy who wore a hat like that one night when he gave me a ride home from a party. I would probably laugh out loud at him under normal circumstances, but I'm wasted at this point and for some reason we have chemistry. I excuse myself from the conversation, leaving Sara in a conversation threesome with the hottie and the creep. As I make my way over to him, he's watching me move through the room. It immediately turns me on.

"Hey," I say. "How are you?"

"Good," he says. "A little wasted though."

"Hey, me too," I reassure him. I reach out my hand. "I'm Erika."

"Heath," he says, a drunk grin on his face. I'm not sure if it's me or the booze putting it there.

"So how old are you, Heath?" I ask. He looked younger and younger the closer I got to him.

"I'm 27," he says. "Why?"

Oh yikes, to be 25 again, drunk in a bar in Wisconsin. I'm pretty sure I never did that when I was that young. I was already too busy with my babies then. I was actually probably practicing trying to get pregnant with my daughter, waiting out the days when the fluids were perfect for mixing together the DNA to produce a girl.

"Hmm," I say. "You look pretty young. I just might have to card you."

He looks at me a little longer, wondering if I'm serious.

"Are you kidding me?" he says. "You're carding me? I just met you. What exactly do you think is going to happen here?"

"I don't know," I tell him, "But I've got a 7 plus-or-minus rule, and if you're only 27 then you're out of my range."

Just after I'd moved into my new house, I read an article in Cosmopolitan about age differences in relationships. Ironically, it was weeks before I met John. One afternoon, I was wasting time at my desk before I had to leave for a meeting when an ad for a Cosmo article showed up in Facebook. Those damn ads get me every time. The display line was, "The Age Gap: A 7 Plus or Minus Rule," and it intrigued me. The article basically said that if your partner is seven years older or younger than you, then you're probably incompatible. There were all kinds of reasons and logic and practicality wrapped around the theory, and basically, it just made sense to me. The only thing I could think of that might be an exception to the rule was music, how music pulls people together, linking generations of people, no matter their differences. It immediately made think of John and our night of 'Broken Wings.'

"Well, how old are you?" he asks.

I pause, having to think for a moment, wondering if he wants to know how old I feel, or how old I actually am.

"I'm 35," I say, pausing again for his reaction, but he says nothing. "Almost divorced, three kids, small town girl all my life," I tell him.

He looks at me sternly.

"Well, 27 is pretty close to your rule," he says. "And what kind of stupid rule is that anyway?"

"Oh, I don't know. It's not really a rule. It's more like a guideline," I tell him.

He leans forward in his chair, taking his wallet out of his back packet.

"I can't believe you're carding me," he says.

"Well, you don't have to show it to me if you don't want to," I tell him, looking at his wallet when I say it. "But I'm not going anywhere with you if you don't."

He grabs his license out quickly then, and shows it to me. Sure enough, he's 27, almost 28. Damn, I was hoping it wouldn't be that easy. Sara starts walking over from the bar.

"My friend is on her way over. Just warning you," I say, turning to her as she approaches.

"Hey there," I say. "Sara, this is Heath."

"Well, nice to meet you, Heath," she says. "Were you at the game today?

"I was, actually," he says. "Great game, huh?"

"Except for the unruly Packer fans we had sitting by us," she says. "They're not the best losers."

"Yeah, they were pretty bad by us, too," he says, smiling at me while he says it.

"Hey," she says. "Are you ready to go?"

"Hmm, I'm not sure," I tell her. "I might stay here for a little while longer."

"Well, I'm really tired," she says. "Do you mind if I go back without you?"

"No, that's fine," I say.

I look at Heath, trying to gauge his reaction. He's happily surprised, I think.

"Let me call you a cab," he says, grabbing out his cell phone.

He calls a cab company for Sara and they tell him they are already waiting out front. We all get up to walk outside.

"Ok, lady," I say, giving her a hug as she climbs in the taxi. "Are you sure you're going to be alright?"

"Yeah, I'll be fine. You be careful," she says, looking at me.

She looks at Heath.

"You'll make sure she gets home OK, right?"

"Yes, I will," he says, nodding.

I lean into him. I have no idea what in the hell I am doing, but it just feels right, and I'm going with it.

As we watch the taxi drive away, Heath grabs my hand and pulls me around the side of the building. We're inches away from each other's faces when he puts his hands on my face and leans in to kiss me, softly at first and then I make it harder.

"Hmm," I say. "That was nice."

"Let's go back to my camper," he says, grabbing my hand again.

"What camper?" I ask. "You're staying in a camper tonight?"

"Yeah, my friend's dad parked his RV in Kmart parking lot and then we've got another pop-up camper too," he says.

"OK," I say reluctantly, suddenly not sure what I've gotten myself into.

We walk a couple of blocks, just talking about where we're from, our families, our lives. When we get to the RV, he stands beside the door and turns to me. I'm shivering, more nervous about being with him than from the cold.

"Do you want to go inside?" he asks, looking me directly in the eyes.

"Sure," I say, looking back at him.

He turns the knob on the door and grabs my hand as we move up the stairs. It's dark inside, but I can still see the layout. There is a pull-out bed straight ahead and the driver and passenger seat are to the right, wide open spaces. He tells me that the door on the opposite end is a bedroom, and the other door is to a bathroom that doesn't work.

"My friend's dad is sleeping in that bedroom," he whispers to me.

"OK, so what are we doing in here?" I whisper back.

"Well, you said you wanted to come inside," he says, grabbing me and pulling me close, trying to warm me up.

I pull back from him and put my hands at his sides. He leans in and kisses me softly on the lips, then probing with his tongue. I kiss him back hard. He pulls me into him and I can feel that he is hard. I slide my hands down his chest and to his jeans, feeling him. I move up to his belt and try to unbuckle it, but I can't get the latch.

Laughing, I say, "Is your buckle supposed to be birth control, or what?"

He laughs, then reaches his hands down to do it himself. I reach my hand inside his jeans, grabbing at his penis. Yes, he's definitely hard, average length, a little bit thicker than my ex.

I wonder how long it will take me to stop comparing every man to my ex-husband. Dammit. I unbutton his jeans and slide them over his hips, letting them fall to the floor.

I move down over his penis, taking it in my mouth. He moans instantly. I go up and down over him, cupping his balls in one hand, and grabbing the bottom of his penis with my other to help things along. Just a few seconds later, he pulls away from me, stumbling.

"What's wrong," I ask.

"Nothing," he says. "I'm already close. You're unbelievable."

"Well, thank you," I say. "I've only been with the same man my whole life but I guess I've had some practice," like it's an athletic sport, or I get a grade or something. Good grief.

Then, he quickly pulls his jeans up and grabs my hand, leading me out of the camper. On the other side of the RV is a pop-up camper. I'm assuming that it's the one that his friends are staying in. As we get closer to the door, I can hear voices. I'm definitely not prepared for what happens next.

Heath grabs the handle and pulls the door open for me to go in first. Inside the camper there is a woman bent over with her ass facing out toward the door. Her shirt is untucked and she's gyrating her hips to the music overhead. After I take it all in, I realize that she is giving the guy directly in front of her a blowjob while the other two guys watch. I look over at Heath, my eyebrows raised.

"What the hell?" Heath says, grabbing the door and slamming it shut. I start laughing and then he does too. I think he's relieved that I find the humor in it.

"What in the hell is going on in there?" I ask.

His face is confused, questioning.

"I have no idea," he says, embarrassed.

Suddenly, the guy who was getting the blowjob comes flying out the camper door. His arms are flailing over his head like he's trying to hail a cab or something. He tries to button his pants, but he's not having much luck. His boxers are hanging out and his belt is straggling down to his knees.

"What the," he shouts. "What in the hell is going on?"

I turn my head sideways, trying not to crack up at the serious look on his face.

"Well, we were just about ready to ask you the very same thing," Heath says to him, putting his hands at his hips and half smiling.

I'm sure he's wondering what I'm thinking about all of this. Inside the camper, I can see the woman tucking her shirt back into her pants.

"Well, come on in," he says.

Heath looks over at me, looking for my approval. I shrug my shoulders and he throws out his hand for me to go in first. How gentlemanly of him.

When we get inside, Heath introduces me to the blowjob man, named Aaron, the two other guys who got to watch the show, and the porn star herself. Heath and I sit down on one side of the booth and he puts his hand on my leg. There are a couple of Playboy magazines sitting on the table so I grab one and open it up, commenting on the ladies, the articles and the ads.

About 15 minutes later, the BJ watchers announce that they are going to head off to bed. At first, I wonder if they are going together, like maybe they're gay. It would be a bit of a mismatch for their sizes, but what the hell. It seems like anything is possible these days. Then, the taller one heads back toward the kitchen, lays down across the full-size bed with his feet sticking out the end. He pulls the curtain across like he's going to get some privacy. The other one, shorter, climbs some stairs that leads to a twin-sized bed to the right of the door. As his feet disappear behind a curtain, he shouts out a 'Good night' to whoever is listening, and we all shout back.

When it's just the five of us left, the woman abruptly stands up, steps toward the door and pushes it open as she flies out into the cold night. She reminds us as she's walking away that she has to get back to her husband, wherever he is.

After she leaves, Heath, Aaron and I are sitting at the table. Aaron is gazing at me while I look at the magazine, like it's supposed to turn me on or something. Now I'm definitely uncomfortable.

"You want to go outside by the fire?" Heath asks, looking at Aaron and then back at me.

"Sure," I say. "I can for a little while, but then I better head back to the hotel."

I slide out of the booth and Heath follows me, his hand on my back. There are chairs already around the campfire ring, so I grab a blanket that was laying on a lawn chair and wrap it around me while Heath stokes the fire. Suddenly, the camper door flies open again and Aaron comes tumbling out of it. He saunters over by the fire, standing, watching Heath and looking over at me.

Once Health gets the fire started, he sits down in the chair next to me. Aaron starts asking me all kinds of questions, where I'm from, my kids, where I went to college, how old I am, and on and on. Then, he surprises me.

"So do you guys want to go in the RV together for a little while?" he asks, looking at me then at Heath.

I look at Heath. I can't believe he just said it. Even the diplomatic and witty woman in me doesn't have a clever come back right away. I pause a little longer.

"Well, I'm kind of into him," I say, looking at Aaron, but throwing my thumb in Heath's direction.

"Well, I'll be damned," he says, looking dejected. "Isn't two better than one?"

I don't even know what to say to that so I just raise my eyebrows and lock my teeth together. I think about that Boys Like Girls song 'Two is Better Than One' that showed up in my Facebook newsfeed a few weeks ago, but this is a little different concept. I know twos are good for lots of things, drinks, shoes, sometimes kids, but this is ridiculous. I peek at him out of the corner of my eye every once in a while as we sit in awkward silence for a few minutes. Then, he stands up.

"Well, I guess I'm not going to waste any more time with you two," he says to us. "Goodnight."

He turns around, throws his arms in the air and walks back toward the pop-up camper. When he gets there, he flings the door open, letting it hit hard against the steel siding. Then he flings his body around to grab the door handle and pulls it hard shut behind him, creating a bang that reverberates loudly in the cold night air.

"Oh, my, gosh," I say, looking at Heath. "I can't believe he just said that."

"Me, neither," he says, smiling. "He's a little crazy sometimes. Sorry."

"Um, yeah. I guess so." I say, shaking my head.

We just sit there for a few minutes watching the fire until he grabs my hand, softly at first then more tightly. He pulls me toward him, trying to get me out of my chair. I stand up and move closer over to him, then sit on his lap. He kisses me softly and grabs the ends of the blanket to wrap around him. He is shivering so I pull him into me.

"We could move closer to the fire," I tell him.

"Or you could just get closer to me," he says, drawing me into him.

"I don't think I can get any closer than I already am," I say.

We sit there for a little while before he kisses me again. He moves his hands over my chest and then slips them under my shirt. His hands are harsh, cold, but it's exciting. Then the night air rolls under my shirt and my nipples are immediately hard. I rub them gently, then a little harder. I can feel his penis thickening under my legs as he is rubbing me. I swing my legs to the side of the chair, shifting my body around. I stumble, clumsy or maybe a little drunk, picking my leg up and putting it through the other arm of the chair, my crotch directly on his penis now. He grabs at the button of my jeans and unzips them, reaching his hand inside. I grasp for his button and unzip his jeans, his penis flying out of his pants, standing at attention.

"Do you have something?" he asks.

"No, why?" I ask.

"Well, if you're going to sit on top of me like that, then I'm going to have to do something about it," he says.

"Oh really?" I ask. "Like what?"

He moves his pelvis into me, pushing up against my crotch. Oh, he is so damn hard.

"No," I admit. "Do you?"

"Me neither," he says.

He looks away toward the camper, like he's going to use his phone-a-drunk-friend-for-a-condom option.

"You're kidding, right?" I ask, a little more serious now as he's still grinding into my jeans.

He shakes his head. Unbelievable.

"Well, that sucks," I say.

The disappointed look on his face is priceless as I grab the zipper on my jeans and pull it back up, then fasten the button. We sit there motionless, my arms inside the blanket that is wrapped around the backside of the chair. My head is laying on his shoulder as he's leaning into me and I almost fall asleep until I feel him shiver, reminding me that I should go.

"I should get going back. Sara will be worried about me," I say.

I pull back from him and when I try to stand, my foot gets caught in the arm of the chair and I stumble backwards. Heath grabs my hand to keep me from falling down.

"Thanks," I say. "What time is it?"

He pulls out his phone.

"It's 3:15," he says.

"Oh shit, I can't believe it's that late, early, whatever," I say, smiling.

"You can stay here with me in the RV if you want to."

"I want to," I tell him, "I really do, but I have to get back to the hotel. We're leaving in a couple of hours to go home."

"Ok, well I can call you a taxi if you want," he says, starting to dial the number.

"Sure, that would be great if you could," I say.

Then he's on the phone with a taxi company, explaining where we're at and asking how long it's going to be. Within minutes, a taxi is waiting in the parking lot of the bar next door.

"Well, thanks for a great time," I say.

"Yeah, sorry about my friend," he says. "He's kind of an idiot."

"That's fine," I say. "It makes for a good story, if nothing else."

"Yeah," he says. "I guess so."

I lean in and give him a peck on the cheek before I turn and start walking back to the bar where we met. I wave at Heath after I shut the door behind me, smiling at him as we pull away down the street.

When I get back to the hotel, it's dark and I can't see anything. I don't want to wake Sara by turning on the light so I fumble around, my hands moving along the right side of the wall. I hear her moving in the bed and I lose my focus, running my big toe right into the stand holding the TV.

"Shit," I whisper, wincing. "That freaking hurt."

Sara suddenly sits up in bed.

"Where in the hell have you been?" she shouts, looking at the clock. "It's 3:45 in the morning!"

"I know. You would not even believe the night I just had," I whisper into the darkness, shaking my head, a huge smirk on my face. "I'll have to tell you all about it on the way home tomorrow."

"Tomorrow?" she asks. "Why do we have to wait until tomorrow?"

"Because I'm tired, and I'm cold, and you probably won't believe me anyway," I say.

I know she won't believe it because I can hardly believe it myself. I don't know his last name. I don't even have his cell phone number. I've already forgotten the name of the town he told me that he's from. But I've got a memory of one night under the stars in a K-Mart parking lot in Green Bay, Wisconsin, and memories last forever.

CHAPTER FIFTEEN

When I get back to work on Tuesday, I login to Facebook so I can chat with John about last Saturday night, the Halloween party, and the mysterious eyes behind the mask of the creepy grandpa. He's online.

Hey there mister

Hey, what's up

Did you have a good weekend?

Yeah, it was good, busy

Did you get the text I sent you on the way to Green Bay

Yeah

Were you home last weekend

No, why

Well, what were you doing

I was home

Meaning here?

No, home

That's strange. I swear those eyes belonged to John.

So what else is going on

Getting ready to hunt next weekend

Where

Home

Well, where's home this time

At the farm

Hmm, Ok, when are you coming 'home' then

Friday night

Text me if you want to do something

On Friday afternoon, as I'm finishing up some smaller projects at work, I hop on Facebook to see what's going on over the weekend. John's brother Brad is online so I send him a chat.

Hey, all ready for hunting this weekend?

Yeah, getting there

I'm on a 10 day run right now

What do you mean

Worked ten in a row without a day off

Are you kidding

No, gotta pay the bills, ya know

Yeah I guess

So will you guys hunt all week, or just the weekend

Usually until we fill our tags

Did your dad used to hunt with you

Ya, I miss having him out there

I'm sure

Better go, ttyl

Ya, see ya

When I wake up Saturday morning, I can't get out of bed. It's my ex husband's birthday, and I can't decide if I should send him a text wishing him a happy birthday. It seems so simple, like it should be nothing to shoot off a quick note to him. It's not the sending, but the receiving that's the problem. If I send it and he says nothing, I'll be hurt. If I send it, and he's an ass, then I'll be pissed. It's an awkward situation. I know that I don't want to be with him anymore, but he was my best friend for 18 years and I still miss him sometimes, especially days like today.

Hey, happy birthday, have a good day

I sit for a few moments, just looking at my phone. He says nothing. Just like a man, I guess. I suppose his new little sidekick doesn't like him talking to me. I wonder what she'd think of me alone with him. I don't know what I wanted him to say anyway, but I guess just a simple thank you would have been just fine.

Later that morning, as I'm lying on my bed reading magazines and hopping on and off Facebook, I decide to text John to see how the hunting is going.

Get anything yet?

Not yet

Whatcha doing?

Just sitting in the woods

Dreaming about deer?

Yeah, something like that

You want me to come out and keep you company

Not a good idea

Why, we could take a nap

Probably not

Ok, well have fun

Hmm, it makes me horny thinking about John sitting in the woods. My mind wanders to a vision of me bent over, leaning against a tree while he gets me from behind. Damn, that would be some hot sex. Him, in his blazing bright orange, and me, naked as the day I was born.

Later that night, I head downtown to The Saloon. My kids are with my ex so I'll just be home alone anyway. John is probably still around so there might be a chance that he'll show up at The Saloon. When I walk in, the bar is full of people, some that I know but more that I don't. There happens to be one stool in the middle of the bar that is open so I plop down and throw my purse on a hook under the bar. The bartender heads over my way.

"Are you having the usual?" he asks, with a grin.

He's a tall, lanky guy, a few years younger than me. With my newfound freedom as a single woman, we've gotten to know each other real well.

"Yep," I say, smiling back. "What's going on in town tonight?"

"Oh, there was a 50th birthday party for a guy this afternoon and a bachelorette party bus that just stopped through for some girl," he tells me.

"Wow, it's busy in here," I say.

Across the bar, I see John's niece chatting with some friends. She waves at me and goes back to her conversation. After a few minutes, she and her friend move over to a table. When I catch eyes with her, she motions for me to come over to their table so I grab my beer and my purse and head that way.

"Hey there, ladies," I say. "What are you up to tonight?"

"Oh, we're going to head down to Snowball's after a little while," Angie says. "You wanna go along?"

"Sure," I say, just as I see John walk in the front door, planting a stare on me on his way over to the table.

"You ladies ready to go?" he asks, looking around at the table of women.

"Hell yes," Angie hollars. "Erika is going along too."

"Cool," John says to the group. "Let's go."

Next thing you know, I'm riding in John's car with a bunch of women who think he is God's gift to women, the prodigal son, practically a martyr. Somehow I feel like this is a test to see if I can handle being around a bunch of married women who probably already secretly hate me because I'm sleeping with their backup plan.

When we get inside, John orders two beers, hands me one and heads off to chat with his friends. Across the bar I see an old friend of mine and head over to say hello.

"Hey there handsome," I say, with a wink and a smile.

"How are you," he says. "Heard you're getting a divorce, huh?"

"Yeah, in the process," I say. "Should be done in a few weeks."

"Wow, that's fast," he says. "Not wasting any time, are ya"

"Nope," I say. "Just want to get it done and move on."

"I bet," he says, smiling at me and then over at John.

We chat some more about my divorce when he says something I will never forget.

"I heard that people marry for love the first time around," he says. "And for money the second."

What a smug son of a bitch.

"Well maybe I married for money the first time," I say, as I turn and walk away.

Across the room, I see John heading toward the door of the bar. I walk out after him, following him and one of his friends. He seems angry.

"Where are you going?" I ask.

"Leaving," he says.

His friend looks at me, smirking, as if to say that she is going with him and I am not. She steps closer to the side the car, leaning in through the wide open window, marking her territory on John, like he is a fire hydrant.

"Don't you want to stay?" she says, almost pleading with him.

It seems strange, a married woman, there without her husband, begging John to stay with her. Maybe they had been more than friends in the past, maybe they are still more than friends. Maybe everything that has been going on with John and me is just nothing for him. Either way, it enrages me that he is going to leave me here, without a car or a ride home.

"Are you seriously going to leave me here," I ask, looking at them both standing at the car. "You're going to leave me here while you go somewhere with her?"

John looks at me and just as soon as it flew out of my mouth, I knew that it was wrong. She doesn't deserve that. I don't know anything about the woman really, besides rumblings and rumors that had circulated in town about why her marriage had ended. And now I was going to be the center of the town rumor mill with the story of my own divorce.

She heads around to the other side of the car and hops in, the biggest devil grin on her face. I want to just slap it right off. She reminds me of the woman my husband fucked so many years before. I realize as I stand there waiting for them to drive away that I am not over it, probably never will be.

Infidelity is so delicate, so careful, and so discreet. The lies that are told, the little moments that begin so innocently between friends, co-workers, family. A look, a little longer glance across a room. But it all comes back around again. The regret, the jealousy, the betrayal and deception comes back, years later, always thinking of how things started. And no amount of money or grandiose apology or worst kind of revenge, whatever it is, can ever replace the feelings of inadequacy that infidelity brings about. And here I was now, the other woman.

As they drive away without me, I am making plans to take a huge fucking rock and throw it through his back window. Then the good girl in me takes over and I just want to calmly sit down and cry. Instead, I turn and head back toward the bar, colliding with John's niece and nephew who offer to give me a ride home.

CHAPTER SIXTEEN

The following week is my first birthday as a single woman and it just happens to be on a Saturday, so I organize a little sex toy party to celebrate. I figure if I ever start dating someone like John who lives so far away, I'm going to have to add to my toy collection to stay faithful. I invite about 45 women, hoping that if even half of them show up, I might be able to get a free vibrator out of the deal.

I spend the whole day cleaning the house, putting together some food and making sure I've got enough beer to get a bunch of women half buzzed so they find some fun stuff to buy and try out at home. It feels like a housewarming party of sorts, since I just moved into my house in September, and most of my friends haven't seen it yet. I'm excited but a little nervous. I haven't had a party with a bunch of women for years. It scares the hell out of me, really. I've got broken tile on most of my floors, lots of painting to do, and a yard full of weeds, but I figure no house is ever perfect and real friends should understand anyway.

My cousin Alicia and the party hostess are the first to arrive. Alicia and I crack a beer while we watch the hostess pulling out vibrators and dildos and bullets, all kinds of oil and lube, handcuffs, panties. It's never ending. A half hour later she's filled my dining room table with the most stimulating sex paraphernalia I can think of, and then some.

Slowly the rest of the ladies start arriving, including my mom. I'm trying to keep up getting a drink in everyone's hand, but pretty soon people just start helping themselves to the fridge. Perfect, now I can relax and enjoy the show. When the hostess starts her demonstration, the place goes crazy. Ladies have got their hands all over everything as we're passing items around, flipping open caps and smelling them, rubbing oils on their nipples and even taking them into my bathroom for some privacy.

"What in the world would you do with something like this?" my mom asks, the group erupting in laughter as she holds a silver bullet up in the air. And not the beer, either.

I can tell she's already had a few beers. Her eyes are glistening and her left eye is half-closed. My mom is in her early 60s now. She's got silver hair and cellulite, but somehow I want to believe that she and my dad still have sex every now and then.

"Are you listening, Mom?" I ask her. "She's explaining everything before she passes it around."

"Yes, I'm listening," she says. "But I just don't get it."

I figure I'm not going to be the one to demonstrate, or even try to explain, how to use something like that to my mom. Cripes, she never even talked to me about sex or birth control until I was pregnant with my first son.

My mom is still holding the bullet over her head as the hostess explains again how to use it, like she's the demonstrator on a television game show. Then, she turns it on and it starts vibrating and shaking. My mom bursts out laughing.

"I can't believe you put something like this, on this," she says, motioning to her crotch.

And the ladies are rolling with laughter all over again.

After everyone has made their purchases, I've got over $600 of free merchandise to pick out. Sweet Jesus, this is going to be fun. Except that I'm already drunk and I really don't want to shop for my new vibrator with my mom and the rest of my family standing around watching me.

"Let's head to the bar," I yell to the room full of half-drunk women.

Half of them are ready to go, and the rest want to head home. After I pick up a few things, clean up the counters, and the hostess gets packed up, about 15 of us head to The Saloon to celebrate. When we walk in, the bar is full of people. There is a DJ and people are dancing. I stand at the bar and chat with Melanie and Kyle. They dropped by my house just as we were getting ready to leave and I didn't really get a chance to talk with them.

"So, have you talked to John at all," Melanie hollers at me, trying to make conversation over the music.

"I saw him a couple of weeks ago when he was home," I tell her. I want to include Kyle in the conversation but it's just too damn loud. I lean in closer. "He was home for hunting."

"Oh, he's a hunter?" she asks, sounding surprised.

Across the bar, there is a group of guys standing around together. The best looking one in the group is glancing over at me every now and then as I sip my beer. I go out to dance with some ladies from the party and when I make my way back to get a drink, the only spot left at the bar is right next to the guy who has been staring at me.

"Hey," I say, falling into the chair next to him.

"Hey," he says, turning to look at me. "Can I buy you a drink?"

"Sure," I say, smiling at him.

We both order a beer and the bartender brings us our drinks.

"Thanks," I tell him. "What's your name?"

"Dave," he says. "How 'bout you?"

"Erika," I say. "So what are you doing out tonight?"

"Oh, these friends of mine are here from back home and we're just out for a few drinks," he tells me.

"Well, that's fun," I say. "Hopefully you're behaving yourselves."

"Oh yeah, we're having fun" he says. "How 'bout you?"

"Well, it's my birthday and I had a little sex toy party at my house to celebrate, so now I'm out with the ladies," I tell him.

Just the mention of sex and toys in the same sentence appears to put him over the edge because he turns away then and watches people on the dance floor. While he's turned away from me, I check him out. He's wearing a green, long-sleeved collared shirt and jeans. He's clean-shaven with dark hair and square-rimmed glasses, slightly taller than me in my high heels. He's attractive, but not really my type, reminding me of an altar boy at church. My first impression is that he's probably a great one night stand but nobody that I want to date. His hands are shaking. I decide he's either drunk or I make him nervous.

"Well, thanks for the drink," I say as I head toward the dance floor.

"Sure, no problem," he says, his eyes suggesting that he wants me to stay.

I start walking away, then turn around and catch him and his three friends staring at my ass. Oh, boys will be boys.

My cousin Alicia waves at me from across the bar.

"Are you ready to go?" she asks as I approach her.

"Hmm, not sure," I say. "I might hang out for a bit and see what happens."

"With what?" she asks.

"See that guy at the bar in the green shirt?" I say.

"Yeah," she says. "Who is it?"

"Well, his name is Dave. He's divorced with 2 kids, works at the hospital, and he's out with some friends from his hometown," I tell her.

She looks over at him again.

"Well, he doesn't really look like your type, do you think?" she asks. "And what about John?"

"John's not here and he has a girlfriend right now anyway," I say. "Dave might be fun for a night."

"OK, well, whatever," she says. "As long as you think it's safe."

"Yeah," I say. "He's harmless. I can handle it."

I lean into her to give her a hug.

"Call me tomorrow, ok?" she says as she walks out the door and into the cool night.

"Yep, I will," I tell her.

And I hope I've got a good story to share when I do. When I walk back to the bar, Dave and his friends are finishing their beers.

"So, do you want to go back to my place for an after bar?" he asks. "I'm going to make eggs and bacon and toast when we get there."

"Sure," I say. "As long as you can give me a ride home eventually."

He looks at me and smiles, probably hoping that it's sometime tomorrow.

"Yeah, I can do that," he tells me. "Let's go."

I grab my jacket and throw it on. He puts his hand on my back and holds it there as we walk out of the bar. His friends are standing outside waiting for us, all with smirks on their faces, proud of their hometown friend for his catch.

"Where's your car?" I ask, trying not to laugh at them.

He motions to an SUV across the street. We head over and hop in. The other three guys are going to follow us in another car. As we head out of town, I start asking him about his divorce, his kids, his job, and telling him about mine. Before I know it, we're pulling into his driveway. When we pull into the garage, Dave puts the car into park and looks over at me.

"What?" I ask, smiling.

He leans a little closer and kisses me softly. I wasn't ready for it. I really just want to get something to drink so I back away.

"Should we go inside?" I ask.

"Yeah, sounds good," he says, sounding a little disappointed.

He opens the car door and steps out. I do the same and follow him inside the house. His friends are ogling me the moment I step inside the door. I'm alone with four men who probably secretly want to treat me like an animal in a cage at the circus. At the top of the stairs there is a striped yellow cat with greenish eyes staring intently at me, like I'm invading its territory. I follow Dave up the stairs. He bends over and pets the cat on the head. I hate cats. I think about him putting his hands on me after he just touched that cat. He heads down the hall to the right, into his bedroom, and I follow him. He turns and closes the door behind us, then grabs my hand and pulls me toward the bed. I'm shocked that he's as forward as he is. I expected him to be more reserved. He puts his hand on my face and kisses me. My mouth is so dry. I'd give anything for a beer.

"Would you mind getting me a glass of water?" I ask, lying down on the bed.

I don't want to be a pain in the ass but it's going to make things a whole lot better.

"Sure," he says quietly. Yeah, he thinks I'm a pain in the ass, but he turns around anyway and heads out the door.

His bedroom is odd to me, for a single guy. It's a little creepy, actually. He's got maroon satin sheets and a matching comforter. His bed is made of dark cherry wood, with a tall headboard and a full footboard. The walls are a deep red color, along with the curtains. It's very dark in the room, but even in the dark I can see that there are clothes laying everywhere on the floor. Soon, Dave comes back with my glass of water.

"Thanks," I tell him, grabbing it from his hand.

He responds by leaning in to kiss me. He lays down next to me on the bed and starts rubbing my back. I already know that this is definitely not going to work out. I have a moment when I consider asking him to take me home, but I decide to stay and make the best of it. He pulls me into him, rubbing my back and my ass, his hands moving all over my body. I'm thinking about so many other things and I'm really not into it. I hope he can't tell. He grabs at the bottom of my shirt and pulls it up over my head, tossing it on the floor next to the bed. Then he reaches behind my back and single-handedly unhooks my white lace bra, pulling it away from my body.

"I'm impressed," I say. "You can do that with one hand?"

"Yeah," he says, bashful then.

He looks down at my tits and then slides his hands over them, tugging at both of my nipples with his thumbs and forefingers. He moves one hand down to the button of my jeans, unbuttoning it and slipping one hand inside. I have a white lace thong on but there's no way he can get to me without taking off my pants. I slide them down and push them sideways off the bed. I grab at the button on his jeans and tug them down his body. He's wearing boxer briefs that are way too big for his body. In the car ride to his house, he mentioned that he lost some weight when he went through his divorce. He's probably overdue for a shopping trip.

I move down his body to his half-hard penis. He's average size in length and thickness, more like my ex-husband. There's just nothing worse than a man in the moment without a rockhard cock. He's probably drunker than I think. I move my mouth down over him trying to get him there. After a few minutes of moving him in and out of my mouth, he's hard. I move back up his body, sucking hard on his nipples trying to keep him hard. Slowly I work on getting him inside me, but I'm so damn dry. It feels like trying to put a tampon in when you don't even have your period. Finally he's inside me, but I can hardly feel him because he immediately starts going soft again.

"I'm sorry," he says. "I don't know why I keep going soft."

"Does this happen a lot?" I ask.

"No, this is the first time," he tells me.

I'm not sure if I should believe him, but I don't feel like spending two hours trying to make and keep him hard, so I roll off.

"Maybe we should just sleep for a little while," I say, not wanting to make a big deal about it.

"Yeah, that's fine," he says, and comes in a little closer to spoon with me. After a few minutes, I roll away from him, wanting to make some space. I haven't spooned with anyone since I've been divorced and this is not the time to try.

About 5:30, I wake up and Dave is snoring. I can't get back to sleep so I lay there wondering what in the hell I was thinking going home with him in the first place. I could be snuggled into my bed at home right now and instead I'm lying here wide awake wanting him to wake up so he can take me home. An hour later, he rolls over and opens his eyes.

"Morning," he says, grinning.

Apparently he's happier than I am about the outcome of last night.

"Morning," I say.

He moves closer to me and starts rubbing my back, then skims his hand down over my ass.

"Nice," he says.

"Thanks," I say.

He moves his hand down between my legs, rubbing the backside of my space. He moves his hand closer to my clit and finally finds it, rubbing in circles for a few minutes. Usually that almost instantaneously makes me wet, horny, but I've just got nothing. Damn, I'm lying in this guy's bed and I'm just not into him. I don't know why. I want to be, but I've just got this mental block. I think about his cat. I think about his bedroom. I think about his half-hard penis last night. I think about the story he told me of how he cheated on his wife while he was on a business trip. I just know it's never going to work when we don't have any chemistry.

He keeps at it, not realizing that I'm not into it. Soon, I roll over and give him a kiss on the cheek.

"I should probably get going," I tell him. "Do you think you could take me home or should I call a friend for a ride?"

"Are you sure?" he asks. "Don't you want to stay for breakfast? I make great scrambled eggs."

I look at him, reluctantly, and say, "Sure, I can stay for breakfast if you can give me a ride home after that."

"Sure," he says.

He sits up then and swings his legs over the side of the bed. I wish that I could just say no, tell him that I really want to go home right now, but I can't. I stand up and get out of bed, looking for my clothes scattered on the floor beside the bed. We dress in silence and he walks out of the bedroom toward the living room, off to face his friends and lie about the amazing sex we never had.

After I'm dressed, I anxiously walk into the living room, knowing that his friends will be waiting to get a daytime look at the girl who stayed with their friend last night. Dave smiles at me from the living room couch. He looks like he's silently begging me to not out him on his non-existent bedroom performance.

"Good morning, guys," I say, smirking,

The oldest one turns to Dave and then looks back at me.

"Hey, you went to bed kind of early last night, didn't you?" he asks me. "I thought we were going to make breakfast?"

"Yeah, I was tired," I say, looking back at Dave. He's trying not to smile.

"Me too," Dave says.

"Uh huh, yeah right," his friend throws back.

"Well, I need to get home. My kids are coming a little bit later and I've got laundry to do and some work to finish up," I say, turning to Dave. "Would you mind giving me a ride home now?"

"Sure," he says. "Let me throw some pants on and grab my keys."

He turns back toward the bedroom and his friends stare at me awkwardly.

"So, where are you guys all from, anyway?" I ask, not really interested in their answers at this point, but trying to divert their stares.

"We live right on the South Dakota border," the smart ass explains.

I wait for some other more creative response but get nothing. Thankfully, Dave starts walking down the hallway toward the kitchen. He holds up the keys like an Olympic gold medalist.

"Are you ready?" he asks, looking directly at me.

"Yep, whenever you are," I say, wishing I would have had the audacity to tell him that I wanted to go home last night. His fat, charcoal gray cat is staring me right in the eyes, looking like she wants to tell me to get the fuck out of her house. God, I hate cats. And chew. Dave's got both. And, strike three, he cheated on his wife.

We turn and head toward the stairs of his bachelor pad. I silently pray that I'm never in this house again but can't commit to anything as a desperate, single woman. I wave as we head out the door to the garage. His friends wave and say nothing.

When we get to the car, Dave is oddly quiet. I'm trying to decide if he's hungover, or if he just doesn't know what to say. For all I know, I'm just another conquest for the divorced guy who cheated on his wife on a business trip but had so much guilt that he admitted it to her a few days later. I turn and smile at him, hoping he'll say something clever, but I get nothing, so we spend the rest of the car ride in silence.

"Well, thanks for the ride home," I say, as I'm getting out of the car. "Have a good one."

"Hey, can I get your number?" he asks, politely.

"Umm, no, I don't think so," I say. "But maybe I'll see you around."

I shut the car door softly behind me. Yeah, maybe I will. But hopefully, hopefully I really won't.

CHAPTER SEVENTEEN

The next morning, I sleep in until 1:30, hop in the shower and then head back downtown for something to cure my hangover while I watch football at the bar. When I stroll into the bar at 2:57, there are a bunch of young guys sitting at the bar, the football regulars, all dressed in their Vikings best. They are paddling their hands feverishly hard on the bar in unison while the Vikes receive the kickoff. I look around and discover that I am the only person with a vagina in the place. Everyone else is probably home with their families, making lunch and missing the game. I fall into a chair in the middle of the bar as the bartender rambles over.

"How are ya feeling today?" he asks, with a huge grin on his face.

"Oh, a little rough," I tell him, my eyes wincing. "I've got a bit of a headache."

"Nursing a hangover today?" he asks.

"Umm, yeah," I respond. "I need something a little bit stronger today."

I sit there a moment and ponder while he looks at me, then at the TV, and then back at me.

"I'll have an Orange Dreamsicle, please," I say, with pride that I came up with something more clever than a beer.

In moments, I have a drink in my hand. The only problem is that I don't even know if I can drink it. I take a sip. Hmm, deliciousness. I slam it. On to round two.

By halftime, I'm hopping around the bar like a Vikings cheerleader, wishing John was there to go home with me and be my quarterback. What pisses me off is that I know he's at the game without me, watching the real cheerleaders and probably wishing he could go home with one of them. I'd rather be at the game with a drink in my hand and dancing to 'Welcome to the Jungle.'. The whole idea of it pisses me off.

An old friend of mine, Tanner, is sitting across the bar. We've been friends for years. We used to play volleyball together until he hurt his back. In fact, I used to babysit him when he was a kid, which I guess officially makes me too old for him anyway. He's very tall, 6'3" or 6'4" with blond hair and broad shoulders. We seemed to have an attraction, but I've always been married and a good girl, except for a little flirting with him every now and then. Since I've been single, I've tried to stay away from him, especially when we're drinking, because I'm afraid of ruining our friendship.

A few minutes later, he's on his way out the door to smoke, throwing his hand above his head for a high five. I move my hand toward his and they slap together in unison. That's just about the only thing that I don't like about him. He smokes. A smoky kiss is just about the worst damn thing that there is, except for maybe a mouthful of chew. And he doesn't ever want to get married or have kids. But hell, I don't really know if I want to anymore either. While he's gone, the chair next to me opens up. When he comes back into the bar, he strolls over to his seat, grabs his drink and heads over to sit down next to me. His eyes are glassy and drunk.

"So, are you drunk?" he asks, his words slurring a little.

"No," I say, lying. "But you are."

He looks at me with a silly grin on his face.

"I have to close tonight," he says.

Oh, that sucks," I say, looking at him, trying to figure out how I'm going to hang around until bar close so that he can go home with me.

"Do you have to stay open until 1 if there's nobody in here?" I ask.

"Well, no, but I'm guessing that Grumpy is going to be in the bar until then," he says, a little disappointed.

"Well, maybe not," I say. "You could just mix his drinks a little bit stronger to get him out of here earlier. He's already half-buzzed up anyway."

"True," he says, smiling.

We both turn back to the game and watch the Vikes win in overtime. Nice.

About an hour after the game is over, the bar clears out and I'm alone with Tanner. We both order some food while we sit and watch Sunday Night Football and I wait for him to be done with work. Every now and then, we chit chat about the game. We talk about work, my kids, my divorce, hunting. After a couple of hours, he finally has the balls to ask me.

"So, what are you still doing in here anyway?" he says.

"Well, I was kind of hoping that I could take you home with me tonight?" I tell him.

"Oh really?" he says, smiling. "Well, I don't know what time I'm going to get out of here."

"That's fine," I say. "It's only 10:30. I'll hang around for a little bit longer."

"OK, well, I'm going to have a smoke," he says. "Will you keep an eye on things while I'm gone?"

"Sure," I say, as he heads out the door. I'll keep an eye on things alright, glancing over at the beer cooler. I toss my head back and finish my beer.

When he comes back in a few minutes later, he's followed by one of the guys who was in the bar watching the game earlier. He looks drunk but I'm guessing he's probably a little stoned too.

"Look who I ran into outside," he says as he walks by behind me.

"Hey," I say. "How's it going?"

It's a young, single guy from town who spends a lot of his lonely nights in the bar.

"Oh, pretty good," he says, settling into the chair beside me.

"Well, that's good," I say. "I'm drunk and just about ready to go home," hoping that it's enough of a hint that he'll want to go home too.

The guy lays his head down on the bar, like he's going to pass out there.

Tanner grabs the keys inside the cabinet behind the bar and heads back over to the door. I turn and watch him as he locks the outside door, then the inside one. He walks back toward the bar.

"Last call," he says to us as he passes by.

"What?" I say, smiling and winking at him. "It's only 11. We were gonna stay until close." I look over at the stone head on the bar. Well, one of us was anyway.

"This is close," he says, smiling back at me, slapping his hand down hard next to the guy's head on the bar.

"Alright, fella," he hollers. "Time to head home. You can't stay here."

His head lifts slowly like it weighs 1000 pounds. His eyes are red, glassy. Yeah, he's definitely stoned. I think his world is moving in slow motion at this point. He turns and looks at me.

"Will you give me a ride home?" he asks, dropping his chin like a dog that just got scolded.

"Well, where is home?" I ask. I haven't completely ruled it out at this point, but I know that I've had enough to drink that I'm not leaving town.

"I live about 5 miles north of town on County Road 16," he mumbles.

"No, sorry," I say, apologetically. "I'm not leaving town tonight. I've had too much to drink."

"Well, I guess I'll have to call for a ride then," he says, with a voice suggesting I might change my mind if he whines a little. He looks at me for another chance. "Give me a minute."

"Well, hurry up," Tanner tells him, his voice irritated.

The guy picks up his cell phone and fumbles with it. We listen while he makes arrangements for a ride home.

"15 minutes," he says, laying his head back down.

Tanner turns around and starts his cleaning routine, wiping down the bar, emptying the garbage, washing glasses. Then he opens the door of the cooler to start restocking the bottles and cans. I watch him from across the bar, his strong muscular arms moving quickly, the bottles sliding smoothly, one after the other. Before he went inside, he shut off the radio. It's quiet in the bar. And I'm alone with the passed out stone head.

A few minutes later, his cell phone rings and vibrates hard on the top of the bar. I watch him as he lays there, motionless. It rings again. Yikes.

"Hey, are you going to answer that?" I ask, loudly.

His body shakes, then his head thumps off the bar as he grabs for his phone.

"Yeah," he says into the phone, incoherent. "Yeah, be right there."

As he stands up, he looks around the bar in a haze. He grabs his hat, takes it off and rubs his head, not realizing that I'm still sitting there.

"You outta here?" I ask. "Tanner's in back."

"Yeah, I gotta get goin'," he says, stumbling sideways as he heads toward the door.

"Alrighty," I say. "Have a good one."

He turns and waves a hand as he pushes open the door. I turn back toward the bar as Tanner comes back out.

"Already gone?" he asks.

"Yeah," I say. "In more ways than one. He was so stoned."

He laughs, wiping his hands with a towel.

"How much longer is it going to be?" I ask.

"Maybe 10, 15 minutes?" he says. "Do you still want to wait?"

"Yeah, I'm good," I tell him. "Can I get another beer while I'm waiting?"

He knows damn well that I don't need another drink but he grabs me one anyway, opens it and sets it down in front of me. As he walks away, I start wondering if I should be doing this. I think about our friendship, knowing that he's one of just a few guys that I can talk to about stuff, someone I actually get along with. I don't really want things to change between us, but I know that if we have sex it probably will. It's a momentary setback.

"So do you want to go to your place or mine?" I holler across the bar, hoping he'll hear me in the cooler.

Tanner doesn't say anything, or I can't hear him anyway. While he's gone, I think about heading back there and sneaking up behind him. I think about grabbing a beer and ripping the top off. I think about letting the hair out of my ponytail with a dramatic head shake, pushing him up against the wall and assaulting him. Or maybe letting him bend me over a chair while I hold two bottles of beer to my nipples. Like a lingerie model, only drunk. While I'm daydreaming, he comes back out to the bar.

"Did you say something?" he asks. "I thought I heard somebody talking but I can't hear anything back there."

"Just wondering where we're gonna go from here?" I ask again.

"It's up to you," he says, smiling.

"Let's go back to my place," I say. I still wonder if he is talking about the future but I can't see any further than tonight, or maybe getting up for work tomorrow. It reminds me that I have a meeting at 9 a.m. But it's only 11:30 now.

"That's fine," he says. "But let's take my truck to my house and then you can pick me up and give me a ride home in the morning. That way, we don't have to worry about anyone wondering why my pickup was parked here all night."

"Ok, sure," I say, wondering why it matters.

He walks over to the cabinet and turns out the bar lights. There are still lights streaming in from the back room, where the kitchen is, so I don't have to worry about slamming into anything in the dark.

"C'mon," he says, motioning toward the back room. I follow him, hoping that he's going to lead me back to the kitchen and fuck my brains out. There is a huge stainless steel prep table in the middle of the room that would be fantastic to have sex on. It's just the right height so that I could sit and he could stand while slamming his sausage into me. As we pass, I pause a minute.

"What's the matter?" he asks.

"Nothing," I say, smiling.

I remind myself that a restaurant kitchen is probably not the best atmosphere for our first time together, but the thought of it will at least get him going if he isn't already there.

"You pervert," he says. He knows me well.

"What?" I ask, smirking.

"Let's go," he says, motioning with his head toward the door. He waits for me to start, and then follows closely behind.

When we get outside, the night air is cool. It's November and I can see my breath in the air. In silence, I walk in front of him until we reach his truck. I walk passed it to my car. He gets in and starts the engine, then waits for me to do the same. It seems polite to me. I'm surprised because there are rugged parts to his personality, but in that moment he seems chivalrous. He backs out and I follow him through town. When we reach his house, I wait in the driveway for him to put his keys in the house. I wonder again if we should be doing this. I don't want to ruin our friendship and I don't want to break his heart. All I can think about is how this will change everything. I wonder how I will walk into the bar and not think about him undressing me with his eyes.

Then I see him fumbling with the door and pulling it closed behind him. In that moment, I want to back out of the driveway and leave. And then, just as he's walking toward the car, I do.

When I get home, I crawl into my bed, happily alone. In the morning, I should be in a hurry to shower and get to work, but I don't have a meeting until 9, so I take my time. I think about the last couple of days. Dave and Tanner, but always back to John. Before I know it, I'm bawling uncontrollably.

When I get to work, I'm feeling so sad. Then I get a text from Tanner.

What happened to you last night?

Sorry, just tired

That's ok. Me too.

How are you feeling today

A little rough. 530 can't come fast enough.

Yeah, I'm done at 4

Lucky

Have a good one

Hey you too.

I'm feeling relieved that he's not mad at me for ditching him last night, and I'm hoping that we can still be friends. In the end, that's what I wanted us to be anyway.

CHAPTER EIGHTEEN

When I get home from work that Monday, I change my clothes and head to the library for some new reading material. It's one of those things that I love to do, but never had much time for before my divorce. Now I have this time to fill. I'm better than I used to be, but it's still hard to not see my kids every day. I have these days when I get home and the house is empty, quiet and cold.

I look through the 7-day books, but I don't find anything that sounds interesting. I peruse the non-fiction, looking for some self-help something or other that will love me through these lonely days as a single woman. Nobody home but me. With the luck I had in my first marriage, it would have to be something along the lines of "How to Keep Your Husband from Fucking Your Best Friend." That would be perfect. I move on to fiction, trying to find something pornographic enough to turn me on, but disguised as a romance novel. Then, I desperately leave with some trashy novel by an author I've never heard of before.

When I get home, I make dinner for one, open a bottle of wine, and login to work for a little while. After I catch up on my e-mails, I look at the clock. It's only 7. Cripes, if I go to bed now, I'll be up at 3 in the morning. I decide to take a bath. In my master bathroom, I have a great corner tub with jets. I sit on the side of the tub to start the water running. First it's cold, then turning warmer, running over my hand until it's hot.

I go back to the bedroom and grab my laptop so I can listen to music and read my book. A few minutes later, I dip my foot into the water with a glass of wine in one hand and my book in the other. I shave my legs, smooth as a baby's butt now. I run my hands over my body, trying to convince myself that I'm not half bad for a 35-year-old mother of three with stretch marks, cellulite, saggy tits and all.

I try to read a little, but I just can't get into the book. I feel like I'd rather make my own smut book, my own love story. I turn on Jango, hoping that it will fix my heart tonight. The first song is all wrong. I flip the station. The second song is worse. I flip it again. On the third try, I hear Tim Mahoney's "More Than a Moment."

The more I see you

The more I feel you

The more I want you

For more than a moment

I listen as the words flow. The song reminds me of John, the night I first met him about 2 months ago. I don't want to be in a love affair with someone who lives 400 miles away from me. We'll never see each other. With the way that our marriages both ended, I'll never trust him and he probably won't trust me. It will be too damn hard and I know that my heart just can't handle that right now.

At 8:30, as I'm getting out of the tub and drying myself off, I get a text from my oldest son, Bryce. Whenever I see his name pop up on my phone, I feel a little tug at my heart. He's been through so much in the past few months. He went from a happy-go-lucky 7th grader, to a kid whose parents hardly speak to each other. I want to love him through it, but I can hardly function myself. Slowly, slowly, slowly, I'm starting to piece together the inadequacies of my marriage, and it hurts.

Hey mom

    Hey buddy

What are you doing

    Just getting ready for bed. How about you

Me too

    How was your day

Good

    I miss you

Me too

    Love you

Love you too

That's all we've got now, just little moments of checking in with each other when he isn't here with me. I feel like slowly I am losing him, losing my first-born to his dad, like it's a war, a battle, trying to win him over to be with me. But I know that at his age he needs a male role model in his life much more than he needs his mother every day. I know that someday I'm going to have to love him without seeing him every day but I'm starting to realize that it's going to be sooner than I ever expected. I'm resentful. I want Brian to be a good dad, to show me respect, as the mother of his children, so that at least my kids will see that for all the bad choices he's made, he is still their dad.

I grab my library book from my nightstand. I open it and start reading, but I just can't focus. I need a song right now, not sure what it is, but I go back to my laptop and hop on Jango again, looking for something to cheer me up. The first song that comes up is Brad Paisley's "He Didn't Have to Be." Whenever I hear that song, I always throw 'an asshole' on the end of it. Everyone keeps telling me to take the high road, be the bigger person. If that's the case, I'm already a Sumo wrestler drinking a Miller High Life on a dirt road in heaven.

I start thinking about John again, wondering what he is doing tonight, wondering if he could be the kind of man in the song. A man who could love a single mom like me, sweep me off my feet and help me unpack my baggage, loving me all the same. I haven't talked to him since last week when he told me that he couldn't stay for my birthday because Brad and his wife were coming for a visit.

Hey, what are you up to tonight

Just leaving the cities, how about you

Really? What were you doing in the cities?

Just got done watching a wrestling match at the U of M

Fun. Did they win?

Yeah, it was a close one though

You'll be home late

I'm actually staying here tonight

Staying where

Just outside the cities

I pause for a minute, thinking about whether or not I even want to pose the question. I look at the clock, 9:45 already. I pick up my phone.

I could be there in a couple of hours if I leave right now

Are you kidding

No, why

What about your kids

They're with their dad

What about work tomorrow

I can just bring my stuff for work and leave from there

For a few minutes, he doesn't text anything. I start wondering if he fell asleep. I'm so snuggled cozy in my bed right now that I don't want to get out, but the idea of spending the night with John is absolutely thrilling to me. I push the covers back and bound over to my closet to grab my overnight bag. I throw it on the bed, still waiting to get a text from him. I grab my favorite black and white striped pant suit that never wrinkles. It's big on me now but it's the best I've got. Still no text from John. I throw in my 3-inch black snakeskin heels, some trouser socks and a white cami. I still have nothing from him. I'm not going to need pajamas since we're going to be having sex all night. Then, I decide I might as well not waste any more time packing if he doesn't want me to meet him. I grab my phone.

Well, do you want me to come or not?

It's up to you, I have to be at a meeting at 8

Me too, I'll throw some stuff in a bag and leave in a few minutes then

Are you sure

Yep, I'm sure, get some sleep, I'll text you when I'm almost there

You are crazy

Send me the name of the hotel, I'll map the address " when I'm on the road

I set the phone down and race into my bathroom. Damn, I shaved my legs but skipped my pubes. I wasn't planning on an erotic night in a hotel when I took my bath earlier. Quickly, I run the razor over myself, leaving a tool belt on top. I head back to my closet. The worst part is that I've got to put clothes on and I don't really want to. I'd rather drive the entire trip naked and show up at the hotel in nothing at all. I bet that would really shock the hell out of him. I throw on a pair of jeans and rummage through my sweaters. Nothing fancy, since it's just going to come off anyway. I pull out a brown hoodie and throw it over my head, then step into a pair of brown heels already on the floor. I head back to the bathroom to grab my toiletries and throw them into my overnight bag. I pick my cell phone up off the bed and head out to the kitchen to grab some nourishment for the long night ahead of me.

When I get outside, I realize that I forgot my laptop. I head back into the house, into my room, grab the laptop and out the door. The second time, I realize that I forgot my briefcase with the contract that I need for work tomorrow. Cripes, I wonder if I am the only woman in the world who has to go back for things that she's forgotten. Keys, phone, myself. As I'm getting into my car, I get a text from John with the name and address of the hotel. By the time my car is finally backing out of the driveway, it's 10:03. I'm already wet and I haven't even laid eyes on him.

The drive is easy. It seems to take forever, but goes fast. I don't know how to explain it. I have always liked to just get in the car and drive, turn on the radio with no particular place to go. When I was young, my dad had an old GMC pickup that he would use to haul things to the compost pile or just take a drive out to visit his widow mom. Sometimes he would let us go along and other times he would go alone. The truck had an old floor shift and I loved to watch his leg move up and down as he moved through the gears. When I was fourteen, he taught me how to drive it myself and when I got good enough, I would take it out on the weekends when my parents were gone for a few hours. I would just drive the back streets, trying to avoid the only cop in town, but still going far enough to see what was going on. I would manual down the windows and crank up the old radio that blared white noise on all but two stations, belting out tunes while my long curly hair fluttered in the breeze.

Tonight, it's mid-November but I have my window down, the early winter wind blowing harsh across my face to keep me awake. There is life all around me, everything is moving, but the movement seems futile, mindless. It feels like I am in one of the best moments of my life, yet I haven't experienced it. It's the anticipation of it. I think that's how I always imagined it to feel. Along the way, I wonder if any good will ever come of me and John.

When I was a 17, I read a book about a torrid love affair between a man and a woman whose lives made it impossible for them to be together with any success at all. He was a Nazi soldier and she was a Jew, but somehow, in some crazy moment in a concentration camp, their lives had slammed together in passion. He would leave his home at night when he wasn't working and meet her in obscure places inside the camp. They made love everywhere. Being caught would certainly send them both to their graves. But they did it anyway. I can't even remember the name of the book anymore, but the story has stayed with me forever.

As I drive into the city lights of Minneapolis, I want to text John to tell him where I am, but I decide to just keep driving. He's probably sleeping anyway, and there's no reason to wake him up until I am almost there. I pass exit after exit, thinking about what will happen when I get there. I hate the song on the radio, so I fumble with the station until I find 'Always Be My Baby,' by Mariah Carey. It's my baby song for my oldest son because it was popular when I was pregnant with him and it always makes me smile. I sing along and get lost in the moment as tears well in my eyes, my mind wandering and wondering how I got to this place in my life, driving two hours to meet a man just to have sex in a hotel room. It feels like that's all we are.

Suddenly, the navigation on my phone lights up the darkness inside the car and scares the hell out of me. It tells me that my exit is approaching in 3 miles, stay to the left. I decide to send John a quick text as I approach the exit.

Hey, are you awake, I'm almost there

A few minutes passes without a response. I guess that's a no. As I head up the ramp, the navigation tells me to take a right, then another right. I head down a frontage road toward a shopping mall with some restaurants and a gas station. I see some other hotels, but not the one where John is staying. I keep going until I reach a stop light and presume that I am lost. Waiting at the red light, I send him another text.

I think I'm lost

He says nothing. That's just great. I'm lost trying to track down the hotel for a tryst with my lover, friends with benefits, or whatever it is, and he's sleeping right through it. Then, my phone lights up, like the proverbial beacon in the night.

Hey, where are you

Were you sleeping

Yeah, I had a little nap

I'm over by Super America

What, where

I think I took the right exit, I just passed McDonald's now

Oh, I think you turned off too soon

Well now what am I supposed to do

Go straight through the next set of lights and take the road around to the left

What's the room number

115

OK, see you in a bit

I follow John's directions and a few minutes later I am pulling into the parking lot of the hotel. I have a huge smile on my face as I send him a text.

I'm here

I roll out of my car, throw my bag over my head and head toward the front door of the hotel. When I step inside, there is a woman standing at the front desk, pretending to look busy. As I cross the lobby, I turn my head and see John standing in the middle of the hallway with his hands hanging on his hips and a huge smile on his face. He looks absolutely handsome in a pair of perfect-fitting jeans and a maroon dress shirt, a black belt and black dress shoes. I want him to turn around so I can see his ass in them but I decide I'd rather take them off and see the real thing. I try to saunter toward him like a

Hollywood heroine greeting her hero, but all I feel is clumsy. As I get closer, he starts shaking his head at me, in disbelief at my pure shamelessness for just wanting to be with him. I'm standing there with my head cocked to the left, like I do when I'm nervous.

"What's so funny?" I ask.

"You," he throws out with a sexy smile.

"Why?" I ask.

"Your unbelievable," he says with huge eyes in disbelief.

"Why, I told you I would drive here," I say.

"You have to be to work at 8 tomorrow," he reminds me.

"So do you," I shoot back at him with a smirk.

I turn and push open the door and he follows close behind me. When I step inside the room, the sheets on the bed are already torn off. I stop in the living area, hang up my suit next to the dress clothes that he has set out for tomorrow. When I turn around to say something to John, he grabs me from behind in haste, pulling me backwards into him. Oh God, it turns me on that he wants me. It's been weeks since I've seen him, over six since we've had sex. His cock is already hard, pressing against my backside.

"Nice," I whisper, reaching my hand around to get a closer feel.

Saying nothing in return, he wraps his arms around my midsection, keeping me close. It feels so good to have him hold me again. I just want to stay there for a moment. He leans his head in and kisses me softly on the right side of my neck as I tilt my head, giving me goose bumps that spread down my neck and into my arms. Alright, that's it. My overnight bag is still hanging across my body, and it's got to come off. I move briskly away from him and over toward the couch, lifting the bag up over my head and setting it on the sofa. As I turn around, he's watching me move back toward him. I feel like I could have an orgasm without him even putting a finger on me.

"Get back over here," he says, grinning.

Oh damn, this is so hot. It's the first time we've had sex sober, but I feel like I am drunk. I walk right into him, wanting to press him up against the wall. I move into his face, kissing him softly at first, then harder, with appetite. I have my hands on his chest, then move toward the middle to the buttons on his shirt. I start at the top, working my way down. I do it slowly, feeling how badly we both want it, knowing the craving the moment is creating between us. When I get to the bottom, I open my eyes. John's eyes are looking at me. I slide my hands inside his shirt and push it off, flinging it off toward the sofa.

"Let's get these clothes off of you," he says, grabbing the bottom of my sweater, pulling it up over my head and tossing it in the same direction. My hot pink bra shows up in the darkness.

"You remembered," he whispers, moving closer to my face. "I love it."

I turn around again and press my ass against him, reaching around to unhook my bra. My tits spill out of it. He grabs the straps and throws it aside, then cups them in his hands. My nipples are so hard that they hurt. He rolls them hard between two fingers for a moment and I gasp. He moves his hands down over my belly and inside my jeans, reaching inside my panties. If he moves any lower, he's going to know how wet I am so I turn quickly around, grabbing at the buckle on his belt, slipping the button through the hole on his jeans, then sliding down the zipper. He returns the favor on mine. While I'm kicking off my jeans, he moves over toward the bed and lays down, wearing only his boxer briefs with his hands over his head looking like he's ready to get ransacked. I try hard not to smile but he just looks so damn sexy. I just want to be slow, methodical, remembering the little moments between us. For some reason, I feel like this is going to be our last night together, forever.

I still have my pink panties on when I slither up on the bed and straddle him, grinding myself into him and grabbing his arms with my hands.

"Can I ask you something?" I ask.

"Hmm," he murmurs. "That depends on what it is."

I pause for a moment.

"I don't like that answer. I should be able to ask you anything," I say.

He stops pushing at my hips, just staring me straight in the eyes, looking concerned at what I am about to ask. As if I'm going to ask him something grossly irrational.

"Was it you dressed in the old man costume at the Halloween party?" I ask.

He tilts his head sideways, looking coy.

"What are you talking about?" he asks.

"There was a couple there, both dressed in masks and bibs like an old man and an old woman," I tell him. "I swear it was you, your eyes."

I smile, reassuring him that I'm not mad if it was. I just want to know.

"No," he tells me, straight-faced. "I told you I was home then, remember?"

I look hard at him then, unbelieving, but then remind myself that in the whole grand scheme of things, it just doesn't really matter.

"Yeah, I remember," I say. "I just don't know if I believe you or not."

He's still watching me, waiting for me to say something. In a moment, I slip my panties off and pull at the waistband of his, roll them down over his legs. I come back up to his penis, taking just the tip in my mouth, sucking on it hard, then moving down over the whole shaft to the base. John is big, long, thick, but I can still take all of him in my mouth.

John's moans confirm that I'd probably get a passing grade if this was a test. I always think about things that way. Pass or fail, As and Bs, even now as a grown woman. As I feel him close to orgasm, he grabs me under my arms and pulls me up over him. I hold the bottom of his shaft and slowly slide him into me.

"Oh, my God," I utter, breathless.

He grabs at my hip bones and pulls and pushes me, moving me faster in a rhythm. I lean in to kiss him on the mouth, then move over to his earlobe and neck. My hands move down to his nipples, which are erect. In the moment I want to bite one, thinking about him twisting my nipples just a few minutes before. I do, but not hard, just playfully. His back arches a little.

"What are you doing?" he asks.

"Just playing a little," I tell him, laughing coyly.

"Shhh," he says, putting one finger over my mouth.

"Why?" I ask. "Why do we have to be quiet?"

"My co-worker is in the room next door and I really don't want her to hear us," he admits.

'Hmm, that makes me want to get loud," I say.

"No," he whispers in a more serious tone. "Don't."

I'm sure he knows it just turns me on when he tells me not to. I push off his chest and take all of him again, moving faster until he's so close. All of a sudden, I shudder, not from orgasm but just from being cold. I can tell that John is tired. I am too, but I know that I won't sleep anyway. I don't want to waste our time together. I keep moving over him, up and down, slow to fast, reading his face to see where he's at.

Finally he says, "If you keep that up, I'm going to lose it."

Oh well, that's exactly what I'm going to do then. Minutes later, I'm watching him as he orgasms. I try to stay on but he slides me off in agony. When I come back from the bathroom, he's lying on his stomach, either sleeping or trying to be. I lean over and kiss him gently on the cheek. His eyes open and he smiles, closing them again.

"What time do you have to get up?" he asks me, grabbing his phone to set the alarm.

"Probably 6:30," I tell him.

"Are you sure that's enough time?" he asks.

"It doesn't take me long," I say, already dreading having to leave in just a few hours. "I'll go with my hair wet."

He sets the alarm, kissing me and then spooning with me. I grab his arms and we hold each other for a little while. Then he rolls away from me. Before long, his body starts to rise and fall and I know that he is asleep. I pull the covers a little tighter over me, settling in for a long night of insomnia ahead.

A couple of hours pass. I drift in and out of sleeping, but never for very long. As I lay there, I think about how crazy all of this is. I don't know how, or really even when, but I am already falling in love with a man I just met two months ago. I lay there wondering if he feels the same. Occasionally I look over at him, watching him sleeping, face down with his head resting on his arms. It just feels so easy, so right when we're together. I run my feet up and down his leg, secretly hoping that it might wake him so we can have sex again. After a few brushes, one of his eyelids lifts open. I smile and he smiles back.

"I can't sleep," I whisper.

"What's the problem?" he asks, half awake and not convincingly concerned.

"I don't know," I admit. "I really haven't slept well since I moved into my new house."

"Oh, I see," he says, probably not really knowing what else to say, closing his eyes again.

I move my hand over to his back and start scratching, softly. For a moment, I think about my parents, watching my mom scratch my dad's back, softly at times, but mostly just plain hard, leaving red marks all over him. I want him to take me again, but I know that he needs his sleep. I slide my hand up to the back of his head and scratch there too, moving my fingers through his hair.

"You're not going to let me sleep, are you?" he asks.

"Eventually," I tell him.

He rolls over and swiftly gets on top of me, kissing me hard on the mouth. He's already hard and it makes me wet just thinking about having him inside me. He moves down to my tits, taking each nipple in his mouth and lapping his tongue over them. He moves down my belly. I open my legs a little and he kisses me at the very top. Only a damn kiss and I'm writhing on the bed. What a tease. He leaves to move back up my body, kissing both of my nipples again. I grab his penis a little forcefully. My legs are wide open, and I tug him inside of me. He pushes himself all the way in.

"Oh, wow," he says.

"I know," I respond.

There is just something so right about this. Without thinking, my eyes close and my hands go up over my head as he starts into his rhythm. Slow, then a little faster, back to slow again. I put my hands back down and wrap them around his back, pulling him closer to me. With my hands on his ass, I push him into me. He goes and goes. I get so close to orgasm, more than once, but never quite there. I feel so relaxed. I'm in the moment. I just keep losing it. I think he knows I'm frustrated, so he speeds up and finishes without me, which is fine. Someday I'll be able to do that again. I love just being here, with him, doing whatever it is that this is between us. He kisses me gently on the cheek before he rolls over on his side.

This time, I can sleep and I do, until the alarm goes off at 6. John stretches out his arms and grabs his phone to shut off the alarm. I lay there for a few minutes before I move my feet toward the end of the bed and head to the shower. When I get in the bathroom, my hands are shaking as I lean over to turn on the water. I'm so nervous, anxiety comes over me because I don't want to leave. While I shower, I sing.

First, it's the Ferras and Katy Perry version of 'Rush,'

It's a rush, I can't explain,

Like you shot something crazy into my veins,

And I'm ten feet off the ground,

And I don't want to come back down, come back down

When I can't remember any more of the words, I roll right into the chorus of Colbie Caillat's 'Realize.'

If you just realize, what I just realized,

That we're perfect for each other, and we'd never find another,

Just realize what I just realized,

We'd never have to wonder if we missed out on each other, now

I sing, but my heart is half into that one. I need something peppier, a good morning song, so I settle on Mel McDaniels' 'Baby's Got Her Blue Jeans On,' because it reminds me of something that John's dad would like. I sing into the soap bar, rolling my hips and my other arm over my head, while the hot water spills over my body.

Down on the corner, by the traffic light

Everybody's lookin' as she goes by

They turn their heads and watch her 'til she's gone

Lord have mercy, baby's got her blue jeans on

As I turn the knob on the shower, I hear John's voice out in the bedroom, so I guess he probably overheard my singing. When I get out of the shower, I try to be fast so that John doesn't think I'm high maintenance. I brush my teeth, throw some product in my hair and head back out to the bedroom so that he can have the bathroom. He's laying on the bed, looking at his phone. As I walk across the room toward him, he lifts his head and is watching me with a huge smirk on his face. His eyes on me make me want to climb all over him, make both of us moan. But I know that he has to get to work, and so do I.

"Good morning, sunshine" I say, smiling.

"Good morning," he says, a formality in his voice, like he's getting on his game face for work.

"I'm all done in the bathroom if you want to shower," I tell him.

"Yeah, I will in just a minute," he says, still looking at his phone.

As I'm getting dressed, he gets up from the bed and passes by me, without a kiss, without saying a word. When he gets to the bathroom, I can hear the sound of him blowing his nose and it makes me smile. He blows it hard, without reservation that we've only known each other a couple of months. Over on the desk I see a clip with a wad of money inside it. As I step closer, I see a bunch of 100 dollar bills. It seems strange to me that he would leave it just lying out there that way, like it's a test for me to slip one out of it and buy myself a little something, almost an invitation. I'm over by the desk as John comes out of the bathroom, rummages through his bag and heads back toward the bathroom.

"I'm probably going to be gone by the time you get out of the shower," I say, walking toward him.

"Alright," he says, grabbing my arm and pulling me closer.

"Can I have a kiss?" I ask.

He leans into me, pecking me on the cheek. He hasn't brushed his teeth yet, so that's all I'm going to get. Damn. He turns around and closes the door behind him. I finish getting dressed, slipping my suit coat on last. Then, I gather up my things, throwing them into my bag and head out the door of the hotel room, softly shutting it before I head down the hallway toward the lobby. As I'm walking away, I feel like someone is watching me, but when I turn around, no one is there. Hopefully it wasn't one of his co-workers. I'm sure I'm not the first woman John has invited to his hotel room while on a business trip, and I probably won't be the last, even though I would like to be. At 7, I push open the door of the hotel into the cool brisk morning and shuffle toward my car.

About 15 minutes later, I grab my phone to text John.

We should have fucked before I left

Well come back then

I would if I didn't have a meeting at 830

I'm supposed to be in a meeting with my team, but by the time I park my car and roll in the door, it's 8:35. By the look on my manager's face, she's not thrilled with me. Besides the fact that I'm late, my face is beaming from the events of the past 12 hours, and even the hardest slap couldn't clear it from my face.

CHAPTER NINETEEN

On the way back to our offices, I want to tell my closest friend at work about my night with John, but all I do is listen as she talks about her daughter and the birthday party that she had for her over the weekend. The food and the decorations and the guest list. All I hear is blah, blah, blah. I've already given up on the whole birthday party bigger than my budget thing. When we get back to our offices, we go our separate ways. I hook up my laptop to my docking station and login.

A few minutes later, my co-worker interrupts my fairytale moment by hollering over to the top of the cubicles.

"So, how was your birthday party this weekend, anyway?" she asks.

"Oh, fine," I say, not wanting to get into the details with her.

Something in my vague answer must have sparked her interest because she scares the hell out of me when she is standing beside my office chair. I look over at my monitor to confirm that I don't have anything ridiculous popping up, like "How to Catch and Keep the Man of Your Dreams."

"Wait, what? What do you mean, fine?" she asks, smiling, her hands on her hips. "Didn't you have a sex toy party on Saturday?"

"Yeah, I did," I say. "We had a great time. I earned over 600 bucks in free stuff that I have to finish picking out. Then, we went to the bar."

After my night with John, I almost forgot about the weekend I just had. My voice must have sounded like there was something more.

"And?" she asks.

"And what?" I say.

"What else?" she asks.

"Well, I kind of went home with a guy," I say.

"What happened?" she asks.

"After the party, a bunch of us went to the bar and I met this guy. He bought me a drink and then I went home with him," I tell her.

"Wow," she says, sounding surprised.

"Well, that's not all," I say. "Last night I drove to the Cities to meet up with this other guy that I've been seeing since September."

She just looks at me, almost astonished. Yeah, that's right, you heard me, you good girl. I know what you're thinking.

"Yeah," I say, my face softening. I just can't stop smiling. I've never felt this way in my life.

"Well, who is this guy?" she asks. "Where's he from?"

I tell her a few things about John, where he's from, and his family.

"The only problem," I tell her, wincing as it rolls out of my mouth. "He's got a girlfriend."

"Oh. Well. That's not good," she says, looking me directly in the eyes. "How long have they been dating?"

"I have no idea," I admit. "I don't really ask."

"Well, do you really want to be that girl," she asks. "The home wrecker."

"They aren't married," I say.

"Well, if he's going to do that to her, then he's going to do it to you too," she says.

As I'm sitting there pondering why I even told her any of this to begin with, she comes right back at me.

"I know that your husband cheated on you, Erika," she tells me. "But it doesn't make it right for you to turn around and do it to somebody else."

Now I'm feeling defensive, like I'm being reprimanded for falling in love with someone, like I could have prevented it somehow.

"They're just dating," I remind her again.

"If you don't end it now, you're going to regret it," she tells me.

"I know, I know," I confirm, looking away at my computer screen. "You're right."

"What you need to do is end it with him, now, before it goes too far." she advises. "Then, put together a list of everything that you're looking for in a man, in a partner, and then stick to it."

I've already had this conversation in my mind, making a list, checking it twice.

"He's everything," I tell her.

She looks at me in disbelief.

"Well, he can't be if he's got a girlfriend," she says. "If he ends it with her, that's great. If not, I think you should move on."

Coming from the single woman who has pretty much given up on love and claimed celibacy for the rest of her life, I don't even know what to say. It's all lies and blasphemy, the idea that you can make a list of qualities that you're looking for in a man and actually find it. But as she's walking away, I start making a list in my head. Let's see, his name is BOB and he runs on batteries. That should just about do it. I turn to my computer to open up my word processing program. Maybe she's right. Maybe I should make a list.

White

Catholic

Divorced

Has kids

Has a job

Has a house

No tobacco

A little drinking

No infidelity

In under a minute, I've got the first 9 jotted down. For some silly reason, it seems like there should be 10. I lean back in my chair to consider the last one. I type a few things that come to mind, then consider if they are must-haves or just nice-to-have. I finally settle on the last.

Taller than me

The first one doesn't seem fair, but it's realistic. And it's my list, anyway. It's like a grown-up woman's Christmas list for a man. I never got everything I wanted on my Christmas list, but hell, it never hurts to ask.

CHAPTER TWENTY

Right now, before I can worry about what I'm getting for Christmas, I've got to get through Thanksgiving. I'm supposed to have the kids with my side of the family this year, but I just don't know if I can do it. Every year for the past 10, we've spent the holiday with my in-laws who, any day now, are about to be my exes. It all starts when my oldest son brings up the topic of our plans on Thanksgiving Eve.

"So, where are we going to be going tomorrow, mom?" he asks on his way in the door from school.

"Well, we're supposed to go to grandma's house for dinner at noon," I tell him. "What do you want to do?"

"I don't know," he says, his voice carrying weight in it.

There's something he wants to say that he doesn't know how to, something that's going to hurt my feelings. I already know, with him, it's the tradition, the ritual of sameness, repetition. The traditions of his grandma fussing in the kitchen, and his grandpa's toast for living life to the fullest in memory of their daughter, my son's aunt and godmother who died of breast cancer at the age of 30 so many years ago. His enormous brown eyes are watering now and he doesn't even know my thoughts.

"Well, I kind of want to go to grandma and grandpa's house," he says.

I knew it was coming, but it still hurts.

"Well, why don't you call your dad and see what his plans are," I tell him.

Who knows, he might be planning some secret rendezvous with my best friend by now. He picks up the phone.

"Hey Dad," he says, watching me in case I cry.

"Would you mind if we came along to grandma and grandpa's house with you tomorrow?" he says, then pausing. "Yeah, it's fine with Mom," pausing again. "OK, see you at 11. Bye."

His eyes tell it all but he doesn't say he's sorry. He doesn't have to be. It's the beginning of so many moments when I'll give in to whatever it is that my kids want to do, even if it breaks my heart, even if I slowly kill myself on the path. I decide that for everything that they have been through already with this damn divorce and the selfish choices that their dad has made, that I will do most anything to make them happy. And if they want to go to eat Thanksgiving dinner with the turkey responsible for breaking up our family, then it's probably meant to be. I quietly wonder how other divorced parents do it, the holidays, the everyday kinds of days without their kids. I know there will be a peaceful kind of normalcy someday, though there is a freedom in it too, but always loneliness. I feel like an empty-nester at times, a mama bird on her nest waiting for her babies to come back. Or maybe a mama turkey.

When their dad arrives to pick them up, I give them each a kiss goodbye and ask them to wish their grandparents a Happy Thanksgiving from me. I wave out the window as they pull out the driveway and then crawl back into bed and pull the covers up over my head. And the tears just start flowing. I'm all alone, on Thanksgiving. A few minutes later, my cell phone rings.

"Are you coming to grandma's house?" my mom asks.

"No," I say, my voice cold. "I'm staying home."

"What, why?" she asks. "Where are the kids?"

"They went with their dad for the day," I say. "That's what they wanted to do."

"Well, we were expecting you here," she says, her voice shaking in anger.

"I know, Mom, I realize that," I tell her. "But we're not coming. I just can't do it today."

"Well that's not very nice," she says.

"I know, Mom, I'm sorry," I tell her.

"Well, OK then," she says, snarling with sarcasm. "Maybe we can play cards or games or something later?"

"Yeah, maybe," I say. "I'll call you later, maybe."

Maybe we can play pin the tail on the Goddamn turkey when he brings my kids back home later, the son-of-a-bitch.

I sleep for a few hours before my doorbell rings about 4 o'clock. I debate about answering it, knowing that the kids won't be home until 6, assuming that it's my mom. After two more rings, I roll out of a bed and peek toward the windows at the top of my front door to find my brother impatiently waiting for me to open the door. I unlock the deadbolt and the handle, and pull open the door.

"Hey," I say. "What are you doing?"

"I just thought I'd come over and see the kiddos," he says.

"Well, they're with their dad, but they'll be home be by 6," I tell him. "You want to just stay and hang out?"

"Sure," he says. "I'm pretty hung over from last night so I might go downstairs and crash for a while."

"Yeah, that's cool," I say.

But then we start talking. About dinner at my grandma's house, the events of last night, the kids, the divorce. Then strangely, he asks me about John.

"So, what's this I hear about you and John Montgomery?" he asks.

"What do you mean?" I ask.

"Well, rumor has it that you two are fucking, or dating, or whatever it is," he says.

"Who said that?" I ask.

"I had a couple of people ask me about it last night, actually," he says. "So is it the truth?"

"Well, we've hooked up a couple of times," I say, nonchalantly.

"Well, you just better be careful," he says.

"Be careful?" I say, almost laughing. "What the hell is that supposed to mean?"

"Well, he and his ex-wife went through a pretty nasty divorce," he says. "And it sounds like she knows about you two and she doesn't really like it very much."

"Well, it sounds like she needs to just mind her own damn business," I say. "They've been divorced long enough that it shouldn't matter to her anymore."

"Well, it sounds like it does," he says, with a warning.

"Whatever," I say.

"Hey, I'm just telling you what I heard," he says. "And I know you're not going to like this, and I'm not trying to get in your business, but you better think about the kind of baggage that goes along with being with someone like him."

My heart starts racing, not because I don't want to tell him the truth, but because I don't really know how to describe what it is that we're actually doing. And it pisses me off that he would even say something like that about John.

"You know what," I say, my voice a little stronger. "We all have baggage. Look at mine, for God's sakes. Look at the fucking baggage I have, my ex screwing around with my old best friend. Our goddaughter will probably be his stepdaughter someday."

"True," he says, trying not to smile. "Very true."

"Honestly, I don't think his baggage can be any worse than mine," I say.

He heads down to the basement to sleep off his hangover and I head back to my bedroom. With all this talk about baggage, it might be time to take a little trip somewhere.

CHAPTER TWENTY-ONE

On Black Friday, my mom and Becca and I all head out into the cold early morning hours to do some shopping, before the sun is up, before our bodies realize what time it is. We stop at Shopko for a few things that are on my mom's list, then head to Target for some other things. I don't even really have a list yet, and I don't feel like shopping anyway. By 10 a.m., I'm already hungry.

"Where do you ladies want to have lunch?" I ask.

"It's 10 a.m.," my mom says. "Are you hungry all the damn time?"

I've got a history of being a good eater. When my parents took us out for dinner when we were kids, I was infamous for ordering the queen-sized version of prime rib, medium rare, with a side of mushrooms and a baked potato. And I ate every last bite.

"McDonald's?" Becca asks.

"No," my mom says. "I am not eating at McDonald's for lunch today," like she's got the last word on every decision of the day.

"What about Applebee's?" I ask.

Becca rolls her eyes but my mom's face lights up.

"I don't really care where we go, as long as I can have a beer," I say. "And Becca, you can have ice cream."

"Alright, mommy," she says, happy to be settling on somewhere.

We finish up our shopping and head to Applebee's. When we get there, within minutes we are seated and settling into our seats. The server takes our beverage order, and I scan the restaurant for anybody that I know. Across the room, I see an old high school friend of Janet's sitting at a table on the other side of the bar. She is staring at us like we've got horns coming out of our heads, like I'm the one who was fucking Janet's husband instead of the other way around. I look back to the menu in front of me, then back over at her. Now she's talking to her cute little girlfriends and looking back and forth at us all the while. I'd like to go over there and ask her what her Goddamn problem is in front of the whole damn restaurant, loud and in person. But I'm not going to do it in front of my daughter, and I don't want to waste my time or my breath.

I stand up, staring her down while I do. It's just enough to get her to look away, to back down from whatever shit she thought she was throwing at me. Then, I walk over to the other side of our the table and sit down in the chair next to my daughter. I throw my arm around her and give her a quick kiss on the cheek while the bitch is still watching us. Now I won't ruin my appetite. Perfect, let's eat.

Later that night, while my daughter is in the bathtub, and the boys are downstairs playing Xbox, I sit down on the couch to read a magazine. Suddenly, there is a loud noise outside, like something hitting against the house. It's already dark outside and it's cold, and I really don't want to go out if I don't have to. I decide to ignore it. Then, it happens again. Thud. It sounds like a small rock or a clod of dirt, and it sounds like it's hitting the hardwood siding between the living room and my bedroom. Thud, it happens a third time.

I walk over to the patio door and hit the switch on the light that hangs over the door, but it does nothing. I look up at the light, then hear something rustling in the grass behind where the bonfire pit sits in my yard. The bonfire pit that has never been used. Without a man around, it just doesn't feel right to me. I step out on the deck and look out over the field behind my house. There is a crescent moon tonight, but it's cloudy too so there's not much light from the sky. Off to my right, out in the field behind my house, I hear a couple of voices, women's voices. Then I see a couple of figures running, short, petite bodies, heading to the east and toward the light of the moon. They're running like I've got a shotgun in my hand, their blonde ponytails dancing with their movement. I stand there, my hands at my hips just watching them, still running, all the way out to the field that is barren now from being picked a few weeks back. Cripes, I could get in my ATV and run them down, but what a waste of time.

I head back in the house, lock the patio door behind me, and head for the bathroom to help my daughter.

"Hey sweetie," I say. "All ready to get out?"

She lifts her hands out of the tub and shows them to me, her skin puckering.

"Oh, goodness," I say. "I guess you are."

"Mommy?" she says.

"Yes," I say.

"Mommy, what was that noise outside?" she asks.

"I don't know," I tell her. "Something hitting the house."

"What do you mean?" she asks. "Like what?"

"Oh, mud or a rock or something," I say. "Someone threw something at the house."

"How do you know?" she asks.

"I saw them running off into the field," I tell her. "I don't know who it was."

"Why?" she asks.

"I don't know why," I tell her. "Maybe because people know that I'm a single mom living by myself."

Her eyes are wide, and she's watching my face, probably wondering if I'm scared. And I am.

For the first time since I moved into my new house and officially became a single mom, I am afraid. Scared for my kids, not just from some bitches throwing something at my house tonight, but because without a man in the house, my kids will always have a fear.

Later, as I'm reading to my daughter in bed, tears start brewing in my eyes and a thickness grows in my throat, thinking about the moment in Applebee's earlier in the day. The book is Dr. Suess' 'Did I Ever Tell You How Lucky You Are?,' and I've already read it maybe a hundred times. But tonight, for some reason, it's different. I realize that I really am lucky to be at this point in my life. Yes, a divorce. Yes, an ex who is already shacking up with my best friend. But hell, I've got 3 healthy kids, a roof over my head, food to eat, a car, a job, and a family who loves me dearly.

My voice trembles as I read.

"What's wrong, Mommy?" my daughter asks.

I have to stop for a moment before I can respond.

"I'm just feeling sad tonight," I tell her. "I'll be ok."

She looks me in the eye, then puts her hand on my back, rubbing it. I kiss her gently on the cheek. She watches me a moment and then we turn back to the book, to remind us of how lucky we really are, baggage and all.

CHAPTER TWENTY-TWO

Right after Thanksgiving, my hometown has a festival to kick off the Christmas season. There are chestnuts roasting on open fires, kids making cobbler filled with all sorts of fruits, apples and peaches, even blackberries. And the main attraction is the horse-drawn carriage rides. There are thousands of people who stand in line for hours to sit on the back of a wagon while watching the backside of a couple of horses traipsing through the streets. A local celebrity-for-a-night spews out useless but interesting facts about the homes and the history of our town. The most wonderful thing in the world comes when it snows, precisely about 4 o'clock that day. And it just seems to, every single year. A soft, scenic kind of snow that falls gently, not even chilling as it touches your skin. Every now and then, there's a blizzard with wind and sleet, snow and ice. But this year, the forecast calls for the beautiful kind. Except that this year, I don't have my kids.

For several years, a local real estate developer has held a contest for kids and families to enter their gingerbread houses and put them on display for a vote by their peers. The paybacks are minimal, but just enough motivation to make it worthwhile for some to participate, including our family. For several years, we've entered a house in the contest, doing research, printing plans off the internet, spending several weeks visioning, then planning, design, and finally implementation. The perfectionist in me is never happy with the final product but it's always fun, always an experience. This year, I can't get motivated. It's just one more thing I can't get put together. I want to do it, for me, for my kids, to show them that divorce doesn't have to tear everything apart. But I can't, because the truth is, it does.

The Saturday before the festivities, my kids are with me. At breakfast my oldest son starts the debate about what I already anticipate will turn out badly.

"So Mom, isn't it Olde Fashioned Christmas next weekend?" he asks, throwing a piece of bacon into his mouth.

"Yeah, next weekend already," I say, not really wanting to think about it, about doing everything without them.

"Are we going to do a gingerbread house again?" he asks, with a bit of 'want to' in his voice.

"I don't know," I say, with a bit of 'not really' in mine. "What do you want to do?"

"I think we should," he confirms.

And so it begins, the planning and scheming, but this time, alone with my kids, without their dad. I remind myself that we always ended up in some kind of argument during the process anyway, that it will be better without him. While I'm wrapping up the breakfast dishes, my oldest grabs the laptop and the kids start researching online. I can see him already, making a name for himself in his own right, as an architect or an engineer or something scientifically mathematical, nothing like me, but a master of it all the same. Me, I start daydreaming about John, wondering where he might fit into our doughy real estate investment. His kids are grown and he's moved on to different kinds of family things, college football games, designated driving at the end of the night. I wonder if he's the kind of guy watching from the living room couch or if he'll dig his hands right into the brown sticky goo, shaping it and molding it into the pieces that we need. A few minutes later, my son brings over the laptop, showing me an architectural masterpiece of a Frank Lloyd Wright style of home that he likes. I like it too, but I suspect it will end up in shambles, a little like our life right now.

"I've got an idea," I say, trying to change the outcome. "What about if we build the Metrodome?"

"You mean, where the Vikings play?" my daughter asks.

My sons observe each other's reaction to my plan, then look at me in unison.

"I like it," my youngest one says, the spirit of a true Vikings fan, not realizing the complexity of the task.

"It's not going to be easy," my oldest one confirms in his wisdom.

"Let's do it," I tell them. "We've got nothing to lose, right?"

If nothing else, I hope they will remember my spirit of innovation, if that's what you call it. I go online, find a gingerbread recipe and double it. Then my daughter and I head to the grocery store to get the brick and mortar for our new construction.

When we get back home, the boys are in the basement watching TV, and I've lost whatever motivation I had to make a mess that only I will have the privilege of cleaning up. I holler down at them to come upstairs so we can get started. My daughter leads the mess-making, ordering the rest of us around to get whatever it is that she needs, flour and sugar, molasses, a titch of vanilla. Then, we throw it in the refrigerator to fester for a couple of hours.

While we're waiting, I decide to text John.

Are you coming home next weekend?

No, why

Olde Fashioned Christmas is going on

Maybe

Cool, what are you up to today

Running around

What do you mean

Just doing stuff around the house

I smile while I mix together the glue-like frosting that will hold together our structure, thinking about what he means, like there's some hidden code to his message. What does it mean when a man says he is running around, just 'doing stuff' around the house on a Saturday in early December? I know what it means for me, busy with my kids, making lunch, cleaning up, doing laundry. He's probably just sorting the mail from the week and eating take-out.

After a few hours, the dough is ready for construction and I holler for the kids again. We measure out all the shapes that we need, put them in the oven and impatiently watch while they bake, then cool. Finally, it's time to put together the Metrodome, secretly making memories of me and John all the while.

Before long, we have the sides up, curving slightly around in an oval shape, held up by milk cartons and a whole lot of frosting that is not suitable for eating. We stop to debate for 15 minutes about the seats, what sort of candy to use, the size that is necessary to represent 60-some thousand seats. We pose the philosophical kinds of questions, should they be round or square, big or little. It hits me again that it's just me and my kids now. I pause for a moment to think about, the meaning of us doing this together, as a family, but a different kind. I relentlessly re-apply icing to the corners of the walls, hoping hard that it does not fall apart. We begin again at the decorating part. We've got the turf covered in shredded coconut doused with green food coloring. The scoreboard of leftover gingerbread displays the impossible, the Vikes winning the Superbowl over the Packers in overtime by 3. The kids are busy with the finishing touches when I notice that the walls are already falling, caving in.

"We should take a picture," I say calmly.

"Not yet," my oldest says. "I've got to hold this side up a little bit longer so it doesn't fall."

It reminds me of my marriage, when he would have done whatever it took to keep his parents together. But now, we're just talking about the gingerbread version of the Metrodome. And slowly, we're losing it. I instruct my other two to get closer to their brother. They wrap their arms around each side of him while he holds strong, pride brimming over on their faces.

"Smile," I remind them, knowing that we're just minutes from collapse.

And they do for a moment while I get the shot, frosting in their hair and all over their shirts, as the walls start caving in.

"No!" my oldest son yells, tears in his eyes.

They all look at the structure in disbelief, our work of art now fallen. My daughter starts crying, uncontrollably. My younger son scowls at her, like she's being a big baby.

"It's ok," I say, starting to stir the leftover frosting, making busy work for my hands so that I don't cry too. "We can take the rest of the frosting and candies and stuff and just decorate what we have left. And whatever it is, it is."

I can see in their disappointed eyes that whatever it is, it is not going to be good enough. But we give it a good sport try anyway because that's just the way we are.

CHAPTER
TWENTY-THREE

The following day my kids leave to go to their dad's house for the week and I'm left with the ruins once again. When the weekend of the festival arrives, I don't even want to go downtown, but I don't have anything else to do. I meet my dad and we go on the carriage ride, have a bowl of soup at the community center to warm us up, and a gingerbread cookie for dessert.

Around 10 we head to the bar to have a beer. The place is crowded, busy. People are dancing, slamming shots. I scan the bar for John, thinking maybe he came home without telling me, that we will collide at the end of the night. I have a couple of beers with my dad before he decides to go home. I'm left alone in the bar with lots of drunk, horny people, and then I decide to make myself one of them. And if John walks through the door, I'll be ready to roll.

By 1 a.m., I grab my purse and quickly head out the door, a little pissed that John didn't come home and even madder at myself for thinking that he might. When I get to my car, I just want to call him, hear his voice, tell him that I'm thinking about him. I dig hastily through my purse looking for my phone and dial his number. It rings and rings and rings. I call it again. No answer. I start humming Lady Antebellum's song 'Need You Now,' and hit the radio button in my car. The song bursts out of the speakers. It's the worst kind of neediness, wanting somebody so badly but knowing that you might not be with them, at that very moment, or another day, or maybe ever. I send John a text.

What are you doing

I stare at the phone waiting for his reply, then remind myself what time it is. 1:13 now. Close enough. I text him again.

It's a quarter after one

I'm all alone

And I need you now

Tears brim in my eyes as I contemplate about what I am doing. I turn the ignition of the car, put it in drive and head home to a cold, empty house. Damn, is that texting ever going to seem desperate tomorrow.

In the morning, I mull over the events from last night. I feel bad for texting John so late, and I decide I owe him an apology. I login to Facebook to see if he's online. Happily, I see his name and a green light next to it.

Hey there

Hi

What are you up to today

Just watching football

That's right, Vikes are away at noon, forgot about that

Sorry about the messages last night

It's alright

No, it isn't. I shouldn't have been texting you at one in the morning

I was wasted

The cursor blinks in the chat window. I watch and wait for Facebook to tell me that he's typing something. I imagine some beautifully crafted love chat telling me that he misses me and that he's coming home again soon. Instead, I get nothing.

What else is going on

> Not much

I'm leaving for Phoenix on Thursday

> For what

To visit my sister

> What sister, I thought it was just you and your brother

Yeah, a half-sister I met when I was 26

My dad had her when he was 19

> What's she like

A lot like me, actually.

She's my best friend

She's got season tickets to the Cards/Vikes game so a bunch of us girls are going

> Well that should be fun

Yeah, should be

His brevity tells me that what he really wants to say is that he just wants to watch TV all day and not be bothered by me right now. It reminds me of being married, being an annoyance, a hindrance. I don't want to feel that way anymore.

OK, well have a good one

> You too

Maybe tty

I curse under my breath while I log out of chat, then push down the cover of my laptop with irritation.

CHAPTER TWEENTY-FOUR

The next afternoon at work, I login to Facebook to see if John is on chat. He's online and his brother is too, probably exchanging stories from the weekend. My friend Melanie is online too, so I open a new window. I haven't really talked to her since my birthday party a few weeks ago.

Hey there

> Hey

What's up with you

> Just recovering from the weekend

Wanna meet for happy hour tonight?

> What time

How about 330?

> Sure, see you then

I waste another hour, finishing up a report that I have to get done by the end of the month. Then I pack up and head to the bar. When I walk in, I scan the bar for Melanie. On the other side of the bar, there are a couple of women that I used to work with years ago so I stop by their table to chat while I'm waiting. We exchange stories of what we're doing now, some gossip about former co-workers, and then Melanie arrives, making a seat for herself at the counter. I excuse myself and head over to sit down.

"Hey there," I say. "How was your day?"

"Busy," she says. "Same shit, different day."

"Sounds like mine," I say, our conversation resembling a married couple greeting each other at the end of the day.

"So, how are the kids?" she asks, sounding concerned.

"They're fine," I say, very mechanically, like people do.

"What do you mean, they're fine?" she asks. "Their dad is shacking up with your best friend and you're trying to tell me that they're fine. Bullshit."

"Oh, I know," I say. "We're all dealing with it in our own way. My oldest is taking it the hardest, but it's partly because he doesn't like seeing me single, on my own, doing my woman thing."

"Yeah, that makes sense," she reassures me. "I went through that with my kids too. It will get better."

"I hope so," I say, wanting to believe her.

"How 'bout you?" she asks. "How are you doing?"

"I don't know," I admit. "It feels like every time they come home, I have to hear another story about the two love birds, sleepovers in our bed on the weekends, making pancakes together, drinking wine on the deck."

"Oh, that makes me sick," she says. "I can't believe this is really happening to you."

"Oh, I know, believe me," I say, my voice trailing off, unsure of how to finish the sentence. "It's like a reality show gone terribly wrong."

"So," I say, trying to transition topics. "I'm leaving to see my sister on Thursday."

"Good for you," she says, emphatically.

"Yeah, I just need a break," I say.

"And what's going on with John?" she asks.

"Well, I kind of did something a little random that Monday after my birthday weekend," I say.

"Uh oh, what was that?" she asks.

"Well, I was just hanging out at home, minding my own business when I decided to text him to see what he was up to," I tell her. "He was on his way home after a wrestling match at the U of M, and he was staying in a hotel that night."

"Did you go there," she asks. "Did you meet him?"

"Yeah, I threw some shit in a bag and got in my car and drove there," I tell her.

I tell her about our night together in the hotel and my texts to him last weekend.

"I really, really like him, Melanie," I admit. "I just feel like maybe he's waiting for my divorce to be final before we go any further."

"Well, there's nothing wrong with that," she says.

"Well, I guess I don't really know if that's what he wants or not, and I don't know if that's what I want either," I confess. "Maybe I should just tell him it's already final and see what he says."

"Well, do it, then," she says, like I have nothing to lose.

"Do you think I should?" I ask, not wanting to get caught in a lie.

"Well, why not?" she says. "It's going to be final any day now, right?"

I pick up my cell phone and send a text to John.

My divorce is final

Good, I'm glad.

I'm happy for you.

Have fun on your trip

Thanks

Melanie is watching me while I read our conversation to her.

"Unbelievable," she says. "That's all? That's it?"

"All this time, I've been pushing because I just wanted it to be over," I say. "But now I realize that it's really just beginning. I thought a divorce would help things, but this is just going to be a fucking mess now."

"Yeah, you're right," she says, not even trying to smooth over the reality of it.

"I feel like there's a boomerang that's about to impale my head or something, and I can't outrun it, even if I wanted to," I say.

She takes a sip of her beer with tears in her eyes.

"I want to," I tell her, my voice trembling. "God dammit, I really do. I want to run like hell and never come back, but I know I have to stay for my kids, no matter how bad it's going to hurt."

"I'm sorry," she says. "I'm sorry that you're going through all of this. It just sucks for you."

"I know," I tell her. "It does."

"And you're always going to have to be the bigger person," she says.

"And I'm tired of people telling me that," I say.

"And it's going to get worse before it gets better," she says.

"I know, I know," I tell her. "But someday that boomerang that's about to hit me is going to turn around and head back the other way."

She picks up her beer. It's funny because I'm usually the one giving toasts.

"Well, here's to boomerangs then," she says, with a wink and a smile, and we clink our glasses together in friendship.

"Yeah, here's to boomerangs," I say.

CHAPTER TWENTY-FIVE

My trip to Phoenix goes by fast. On the last day I am there, I login to my e-mail and find one from my lawyer that tells me that she received the papers from the county, and the divorce is final. My sister high-fives me, but I just feel ambivalent. I know that when I get off that plane tomorrow everything is going to change. There will be a churn of paperwork to process for insurance and benefits and retirement accounts, and I'll be dealing with all of that for months and months. It will be real now, and my kids will have two separate households with two bedrooms and two different families, two parents who aren't supposed to love each other anymore, but somehow, even with all the shit that has happened, they still do.

A couple days later, while I'm catching up on things at the end of the day, I get a Facebook chat from John.

Hey, how was your trip

At first I don't know what to say. For some reason, I'm a little scared. I'm free now, in the most traditional kind of way. It is a new time in my life and I know that I should be excited, thrilled to be free, have freedom, but it just feels wrong to me.

Good, great actually, except that the Vikes lost

I was watching for you on TV

Hopefully I wasn't on there, I was pretty drunk

Nope, I didn't see you

We tailgated before the game, it was amazing

Sounds like fun

What have you been up to

The Facebook screen says that John is typing something. The cursor just blinks and blinks inside the text box. It reminds me of the Dr. Suess book where people are just waiting, "Waiting for a train to go, or a bus to come, or a plane to go," except that I'm just waiting for John, waiting for him to say something, anything. Finally, he shocks me.

We broke up

What, why

I don't know, just time to move on

Well, I'm sorry

Yeah, well, it's OK

I've got to wrap things up here and go pick up my kids

Alright

Maybe talk to you later?

And then he says nothing again. As I'm walking to my car, I decide to text him. I'm worried about him.

Are you ok?

Yeah, I'm fine

Well, you seem pissed off

Are we going to do this or not?

What do you mean?

Me and you

I pause, holding my phone in my hand at a distance out in front of me, as if I wear bifocals and I can't see what I'm looking at. It's disbelief. At first, I can't believe that he's actually saying it to me. In contentment, a smile slowly comes across my face. But then, an instant later, the strong independent woman in me is infuriated because I realize that he's asking me out via our cell phones.

I realize that it's ridiculous. For goodness sakes, I work in software development for a world-renowned healthcare facility in the upper Midwest. I love technology like the President of the Best Buy Geek Squad. I owned a cell phone the first year they were available to the general public. But I do not want to be asked out this way by someone who appears to be the love of my life.

No

What do you mean, no

Not this way, not like this

You're kidding me

No, I'm not

Come back when you figure out what you want

I'd like to follow it by, "Because it sure isn't a woman like me." My mind goes fleeting off to some Hollywood moment where I'm shaking my finger at him, rolling my hip and giving him my best scowl, except that I can't because he's hundreds of miles away. And that pisses me off even more, because if he was here, I'd probably just kiss him.

I get in my car, throw my briefcase and laptop across the seat, and hightail it home to my kiddos, musing over John, hoping that I did not just waste whatever chance I had of ever being with him.

CHAPTER
TWENTY-SIX

A couple of days later, while I'm reviewing my Christmas list and stewing over the situation with John, I decide to send him an e-mail to apologize for what happened earlier in the week. I browse his Facebook profile, looking for his work e-mail. While I'm there, I look at old pictures of him, the ones that I saw just after we first met. It makes me want him all over again, not that I ever didn't, but it makes my feelings even stronger looking at him and knowing that I just can't right now. I start to compose my e-mail but I get stuck. I just don't know what to say, how to say it, what's the right thing. But I do know that I want to apologize, so that's where I start.

From: Erika Daniels

Sent: Thursday, December 16, 2009, 3:05 PM

To: John Montgomery

Subject: Hey

Hey there, just wanted to send you a note to let you know that I'm sorry for the way that I treated you the other day. I really just didn't know what to say and it kind of caught me off guard. I hope that you can forgive me and that we can be friends. Hopefully I'll talk to you soon.

-Erika

I surmise that short and sweet is probably the best approach. I strip off all the work crap at the bottom, hoping that it will remind him that I am only human. In less than a minute, I have an e-mail back from John. I cringe at the thought of opening it. Then I do.

From: John Montgomery

Sent: Thursday, December 16, 2009, 3:06 PM

To: Erika Daniels

Subject: Re: Hey

You don't have to be sorry for anything. I asked and you said no. There's nothing more to say.

What do you want from me?

The way that he writes it irritates me. My face gets hot, and I want to throw something at the wall of my cubicle. I push back in my chair and spin around to look out the picture window to the busy street outside a story below me. The cars are bustling past in the cold December air as I consider the question. What do I want from him? I'm angry because I have so much that I want to say to him, but I just don't know how to put it to words. The answer is that I want nothing and everything all at the same time, and I'm not ready for either one. I turn back around in my chair to send what I pray will be one final note. For today, anyway.

From: Erika Daniels

Sent: Thursday, December 16, 2009, 3:10 PM

To: John Montgomery

Subject: Re: Hey

You know what, I don't want anything from you, besides to just be friends right now. You know where to find me. Take care.

-Erika

I wish that I could just leave well enough alone. I know that I need to leave this right now, but I don't know how to, and I don't want to. A few minutes later, I decide to pack up my stuff and head home for the day. As I'm leaving, I run into an old co-worker, a woman whose been through her ex-husband's affair and a divorce and being a single mom, learning to live and love and trust again. I tell her about my life, where I'm at now. Then I tell her about John.

"Well, he sounds perfect for you," she says. "But take your time, girl. You don't want to be jumping right back into something now."

"I know," I reassure her. "But I don't want to lose him either."

"Well, you know the old saying," she reminds me. "If it's meant to be, it will come back to you."

For God's sakes, it's that boomerang thing again. I sure hope she's right. With tears in my eyes and a lump in my throat, all I can do is smile and wave as I turn and hurry away.

I spend the next two weeks wrapping up year-end at work and shopping for presents. I think about John constantly but try to avoid him all the same. For days, when he shows up in Facebook chat, I log out, trying to hide out while I develop some strategy for how I'm going to let him go with the hopes that someday he will come back to me. It is so completely passive aggressive that it has psychotherapist written all over it. Even worse, I decide I want to pick up a little something for him to have under the tree in case I see him if he comes home for Christmas.

Over my lunch hour, I head to the shops nearby where I work. I don't want to spend a lot because I know he already has everything he needs. I just want to make some memories of us. I ponder while I walk, then decide to head to a shop that has souvenirs for the University of Minnesota, from our night together in November. I browse the store twice, but nothing really attracts my attraction. There are t-shirts and sweatshirts, baseball hats, cold weather hats and mittens, pens and pennants. Then, as I turn a corner on my way out of the store, I find a pair of maroon and gold colored plaid boxers with "U of M" monogrammed right across the ass. I know that he probably won't wear them anywhere but with me and that they are just going to end up in a pile on the floor, but they are perfect just the same.

I browse through the store a little longer. When I get to the counter to pay, I have second thoughts. I look at the clerk. She reminds me so much of John's daughter that it startles me, assuming that she might be wondering why I am buying underwear for her dad. It would probably startle her right back to know what I've got in mind with him in those boxers. Somehow, I anticipate the clerk will know just what to do, that she will understand my predicament and advise me, like a college recruiter who can look at your schedule and spit back every hour of every class you should take for the next four years.

"Oh, I don't know what to do," I tell her, distress echoing in my voice. "I want to get these for a friend of mine, but I don't know if I should."

"Why?" she asks, like it's no big deal at all.

"Well, I just met the guy a couple of months ago, and I don't want to be too forward with him," I say.

"Well, they're just a pair of boxers," she says.

"Yeah, you're right," I say.

It's a 12x12 inch piece of fabric that I'll just want to rip off of him anyway, like he's my very own Christmas present. Clearly, she does not understand the dilemma that has formed in my mind like I thought she would. I stand there for several minutes as she watches me silently weigh the pros and cons. He'll probably think I'm crazy for buying him something. Or he'll wonder why I bought him a present when two weeks ago I said no to a relationship with him. But I still want to be friends.

My heart just can't handle this right now, maybe ever. I want to stay unemotional, yet I have a rush of feelings for him that I fear are unstoppable. I think I know what I want and who I want, a life with John. It just feels too soon. I know that I need time, to heal my heart, to live a little, to laugh and sing and write and dance, make some mistakes all by myself, own them and be accountable, be a single mom, recover the pieces of me I always loved but lost over the years. It's a beautiful, complicated thing, the yin and the yang of life. Of wanting to be single and free, but wanting a partner and companionship. Of wanting eroticism, then passionate love-making. Of needing someone at times, but pushing them away in independence too. I know that he needs to be with his kids, and I need to be with mine. I remind myself that life just isn't fair sometimes, that we have to be adults. I feel like this just isn't the right time for us, isn't the right time for me. It's selfish, but true. And I know myself better than that. I know that I will take everything out on him, whatever good he is for me will feel like sympathy, whatever wrong he is will be what I deserve and I'll settle for it.

"I'll take them," I finally say.

She tells me the amount and we exchange monies.

"Merry Christmas," I say, trying to recover from my indecisiveness.

"You too," she replies.

I feel like she's going to roll her eyes as I'm walking away, so I turn around and wave, hoping for compassion from a girl that I've never met before today and I will probably never see again. Oh, you just wait, girl, wait until you're in love someday.

CHAPTER
TWENTY-SEVEN

In the afternoon of the twenty-third of December, I'm the last one in the office before the Christmas holiday. I'm going to be off all next week and I've got to finish some things up. It's quiet, a little lonely. Then, I get a Facebook chat from John.

Ready for Christmas?

I stare at the message, unsure if I should respond. It's not just the message, but the meaning behind it that matters. If I respond, it will evolve into a conversation that will be pulling me back toward him when I'm trying to move away, trying to make space so that I can be on my own for a little while.

Just about, just a few things to wrap up tomorrow

How about you?

Haven't even started yet

Are you kidding me?

No, going tomorrow

Me too, for the little things

When are you coming home

Coming home Saturday with the girls, back home on Sunday

Wow, that's a quick trip

Yeah, I don't like Christmas much anyway

Why

    It's just a mess

You mean, being divorced?

    Yeah

Well, at least you'll have your girls with you

    Yeah, and my ex will be in town anyway

What's wrong with that

    Nothing, I just don't want to run into her

Why

    I don't know, I guess I still have feelings for her

Well, you were married for a long time

She's the mother of your kids

I think you will always love her, just in a different way

    Maybe

Do you think you'll ever get married again

    No way

Really, why?

    It scares the hell out of me

Hmm, I don't really know yet

    On Monday I'm heading to Wisconsin

For what

    Work trip for a few days

Are you going alone?

The cursor blinks again for a few moments, but his green chat light is on so I know he's still around. It always seems like forever when you're waiting for somebody to chat you back. I'd love to go along, just get in the car and drive somewhere with John, wherever it is. I could meet his friends, see how he lives, find out the little things about him, like what he buys at the gas stations along the way, where he stops to eat. Finally, he chats back.

> Yeah, coming back on Wednesday or Thursday

>> Well, let me know if you want some company, I'm off the whole week

>> We could drive to Chicago for the Vikes-Bears game on Sunday

> I might stop on my way through

>> Ok, well let me know if you're going to be coming around

>> I got you a little something for Christmas

> What, why

>> Because I wanted to, that's why

The cursor blinks again. And then, his name disappears from chat and he's gone.

On Christmas Eve, the kids and I have plans to go to my grandparents' house. My grandma always whips up some batches of oyster stew and chili and the rest of us bring appetizers and desserts. Thankfully, I have my kids for the evening, but unfortunately, they are leaving later to go to their dad's house and then I'll be alone. I have no plans for Christmas Day, not that I don't have invitations to go somewhere, I just really don't want to. It's strange how quickly life can change. I sleep in until 9 and then grab my phone to wish family and friends a happy holiday. I send a text to my sister and brother, Alicia, Melanie, a few other friends I've re-connected with. And then I decide to text John.

> Merry Christmas

>> Same to you

> On your way home already

>> Just getting on the road

Safe travels

Thanks

The week between Christmas and New Year's, I just need a break. The anticipation that my life is about to spin crazy out of control is overwhelming. As soon as my ex announces to my kids and the rest of the world that he and my best friend are "dating," my whole world is going to change. I hang out at home most of the week. By Wednesday, I haven't heard from John and assume that he won't be home over New Year's Eve, but I send him a text to find out.

Hey there, what are your plans this week? Are you coming home?

A couple of hours pass and I don't hear anything from John. I decide that his silence means that he's not going to make it home. I send a Facebook message to an old college friend that I haven't seen or heard from in a while. She's married to a wonderful guy, has three kids and a great job as a project manager for an internet development company, living the suburbia life. Her family moved away from the Cities to be closer to family a few years ago, and I see her even less than I used to now.

Hey there

Hey

What's up with you?

Not much, took the week off to clear my head

Did you have a good Christmas?

Yeah, it was OK. The divorce was final a few weeks ago

I had the kids Christmas Eve, then they went to their dad's house

How was yours?

Good, busy, my family came here for Christmas and we're going to Iowa for New Year's

Oh damn, I was going to see if you didn't have plans I would get in the car and come for a visit

Oh sorry, we're leaving tomorrow, maybe all of us girls can come for a visit in February or March

Yeah, that would be fun, enjoy the holiday with your family

Yeah, you too

It feels so desperate, of just wanting to get away from everything. I need a friend, someone who doesn't know about all the baggage and the drama, who doesn't look at me in pity for this sorry damn place I'm at in my life.

CHAPTER TWENTY-EIGHT

The next day I've got bowling, but I don't even want to go. I arrange for a friend of Alicia's to bowl for me and head to the bar around 6. I sit at the bar for about 45 minutes, just chatting with the bartender and waitresses when John's old friend Steve shows up. I give him a big, half-drunk smile as he heads over by me at the bar.

"Hey there," I say. "What are you up to, tonight?"

"Well, I'm supposed to be meeting John for drinks around 6:30," he says, both of us glancing over at the clock.

My heart skips a beat at the sound of his damn name.

"Well, that sounds like fun," I say. "He didn't tell me he was going to be home tonight."

"Well, he should be around any minute now, and my beautiful wife is joining us too when she gets done with work," he tells me as he slips off his coat and hangs it over the back of the chair.

"Yeah, I think he's been in Wisconsin this week, for work," he says, glancing over at the door. "He's here tonight, then leaving again tomorrow."

"Well, speak of the devil," I say, as he walks in the door of the bar, a huge smile on his face.

I can't even look at him without smiling.

He's wearing a double-breasted wool jacket, his bright white smile and tan skin are electrified against the black of the coat.

He's wearing crisp jeans, slightly hugging his strong legs and the curve of his package. I feel inadequate in my ripped jeans and bowling jacket, mismatched in our outfits tonight. As I watch him walk over to where we are sitting, I wonder how a woman does not instantly get wet at the sight of her lover across a crowded room. How she cannot want to fuck his brains out or at least masturbate in the bathroom. I wonder how a man can stop himself from blowing a wad in his pants just thinking about his lover, thinking of her panties soaking from seeing him again.

"Hey there," I say, smiling, mine already wet.

"Hey," he says, pulling his coat slowly off his muscular shoulders.

His friend stands to shake his hand, then grabs his coat to move over a chair, making space for John.

"Here you go," he says, motioning to the chair. "You can sit here."

John gazes at me, his eyes looking for permission or something as I smile nervously.

"Do you mind?" he asks.

At first I just look at him, like it's a silly question, like if he wants to he could just sit right down on my lap and I could rub the back of his head and pinch him in the ass every now and then.

"Of course not," I say. "How was your trip?"

"Good, pretty good," he says, turning a moment to smile at me.

I melt as he settles into the chair, as his leg rubs against mine. If he thinks he's going to be rubbing up against me all night long and then not go home with me, he's got another thing coming. My eyes drop to his shoes. I don't know why, always back to the shoes, wherever I am. It always reminds me that we're all just human, that all we really need is just one good pair of shoes. Yet even in the simplicity of it, I just love shoes and have way too many pairs. Tonight, John's are black, shiny, long. I think about the old saying about a man's shoe size, that it is supposed to be a representation of the size of his penis. Oh damn, so true, at least with John anyway.

While John and his friend are chatting away, I think about a conversation I overheard the other day while shopping for shoes. There were two women, a little older than me, probably in their early 40s. From the other side of the clearance rack, I was peeking through the metal bars to listen.

"I just really like him," the long-haired brunette said, her voice strong, confident.

"Well, what do you like about him?" the other woman asked in a softer, more passive voice, another brunette, but with a pixie cut.

"I don't know," she said, pausing. "Everything."

While I stand there on the other side of the rack, I imagine that her face is beaming, radiant.

"I don't know if you know what I mean, but it's kind of like shoes for me," she said. "You kind of just know if you a like a shoe when you first try it on. It's kind of like that."

Yes, I do know. I know just what she means. I want to interrupt their conversation to tell her that I understand. I realize I'm probably doing it now, beaming, as he's sitting right beside me, as I'm remembering the conversation. Suddenly, John interrupts my fairytale moment to ask if I want another beer.

"Hell yeah," I say, happy that he asked.

As we're getting another round of beers, Steve's wife, Katie, walks into the bar and takes a seat next to me. She is the woman who sold me my house, helped me through the paperwork, the bidding, the emotional moments of home ownership being a single woman on my own. In the process we just happened to become friends.

"Hey there, lady," she says as she falls into the chair.

She looks exhausted, ready for a beer, so we get one for her.

"Put it on my tab," I say to the bartender. "What were you up to tonight?"

"Oh, just showing a couple of houses," she says. "Then I had to wrap up some paperwork."

"You must have had a long day," I say, watching her as she catches glances with her husband across the bar as he and John are talking.

I miss that about a marriage, about a relationship, those moments of just sheer understanding with your partner. The knowing what the other person is thinking without having to say it. The "let's get the hell out of here so we can go home and fuck each other's brains out" kind of glance that just says it all, speaks for itself. I realize that John is going to want to stay here at the bar and hang out with his friends. I just want to be alone with him, selfishly want to have him all to myself. I know that I need to tell him more about what is going on with me, why I can't be with him right now, why I said no to him. I don't want to interrupt his conversation with his friend, so I decide to send him a text.

Wanna go to the Legion?

A few seconds later, his phone starts vibrating hard on the top of the bar. I try hard not to laugh as I watch him. He hurriedly picks it up, reads my text, then turns to me and smiles, but says nothing. I feel like I need to tell him more, that I owe him that courtesy because I've acted like such a drama queen. The problem is, I need time to fix what's broken inside of me and I know that he won't be able to just piece me back together. I need time to find my way, because I'm feeling really lost right now, and he can't be my compass.

We chat a little longer and then some other friends of John's walk in the bar and head over to the table where the other group is sitting. I know a few of them who still live in town, but it's Christmas and there are a few others from out of town too. After John walks over to hang out with them, I stay and talk with Katie and Steve.

About 15 minutes later, Katie and Steve decide to head home and I'm left at the bar by myself, debating if I should head over to chat with John and his friends, or just head home. I know that he wants to spend time visiting with them, probably without me. I decide to head over there for a little while. As I'm sitting there, I overhear John tell one of the ladies that he will give her a ride back to her car, which is about an hour away. I decide to just head home since I'm wasted and John's leaving anyway. I go to the bathroom, leaving my beer sitting at the table so that when I come back I might get a chance to talk to John again. When I come out of the bathroom, the group is taking a picture and his married women friends are all over him. I'd like to grab him and shove him on top of the pool table, tie his arms down, let them all watch while I make good of every last sexual intention I've had for him. Instead, I attempt to intoxicate them with my smile while looking back in agony as I quietly say goodbye.

CHAPTER TWENTY-NINE

The next morning, I wake up at 5:30, cold, shivering. My head is tilted sideways, my gum stuck to the quilt, drool rolling down the side of my face. I'm lying sideways across the bed, no pillow and no pants. I look around the room, expecting somebody is here with me. I remember that John was leaving town last night. I remember that I came home alone or I at least left the bar on my own. My head is pounding, feeling too heavy to even lift off the bed. I decide to roll, colliding with my vibrator lying on the bed. Hmm, strange. First of all, the batteries are still in it. And secondly, it's not like me to not wash it after use. Unless, of course, it went unused in my drunken stupor.

Throbbing, thumping, pulsating in my head, definitely not a typical hangover for me, especially when I drank beer all night. Suddenly, I've got to vomit, but I don't know if I can get off the bed. Then, I'm propelling my body across the room in haste and hurling in the toilet, hard and repetitively. I head to the kitchen for some crackers and milk, hoping that I can keep them down.

Later that afternoon, when I go outside to get the mail from yesterday, as I'm walking through the mudroom to the garage, I notice that one of the coat hooks is sideways. It seems strange to me. I didn't wear a coat last night, so there must have been someone else here with me.

All day long I'm sick. I think about last night, the events, and the sequence. It reminds me of the night in November when I went with John and his friends to Snowballs and woke up feeling like absolute hell, only worse, only sicker.

I spend the day lying in bed, until I decide to quit being such a baby. I get up, shower and get ready. Nothing fancy for a New Year's Eve alone. I head out of town about 6:30 to have dinner at a great little place on a lake, about 20 miles from home. I worked there actually, when I was 15, young and wild and free. My best friend and I, we bussed tables there for a summer. Her grandparents owned the place so we got to hoard leftovers of baked potatoes and our favorites from the salad bar at the end of the night, sometimes even getting the fry cooks to make us up a batch of fresh mushrooms or cheese curds. While we waited for one of our parents to pick us up, we'd hang out on the dock with the kids who lived on the lake, watching them water ski and drink beer in their pontoons. I like to go back there for a quiet dinner every now and then, just to remind myself of that summer.

After dinner, I head back to be closer to home. The kids are coming in the morning and I don't want to be hungover again. When I walk in the bar, it's quiet but there is going to be a band starting around 9. I head over to the far side of the bar where I can see the front door. There's a guy from town, a guy in his late 50s, divorced and maybe as lonely as me. He watches me walk across the bar toward him, conversing with the bartender until I get there.

"Hey there, sir," I say, standing beside his chair.

"Well, hi friend," he says. "What are you up to tonight?"

The thought that he considers me his friend makes me happy. He's been coaching me through my divorce with his great advice and words of wisdom. Life always seems to be better with experience, even the messy kind.

"Just got done with dinner," I tell him. "Prime rib and crab. It was fantastic."

Hmm, the word fantastic reminds me of John, our first night together on the side of the car when I told him so. I don't know why in the hell I use the same word to compare food with a moment like that, but it just seems fitting.

"You going to hang out for a while?" he asks.

"Yeah, for a little while anyway. And maybe I'll even dance if I get enough liquid courage in me," I say, winking.

"Hey, me too," he says.

Just then, the band starts to play and it's too loud to even speak. We just sit there side-by-side, watching the crowd of young guys at the bar and listening to the music, enjoying each other's silent company. Before long, there are a bunch of women dancing, hands over their heads and shaking their asses. After some faster songs, the band plays something that we can actually dance to together.

"You wanna dance?" he asks.

"No, not just yet," I admit. "Let's get another drink first."

He motions for the bartender to come over.

"We'd like another drink," he says to him. "Then we're gonna dance."

Oh shit, I thought I was maybe going to get out of dancing tonight. It's not him, it's me. I'd rather be dancing with John.

"I'd better have a Captain Diet if he's going to make me dance," I tell the bartender.

"OK, you got it," the bartender says, the promise of a strong one in his voice.

My bar companion looks at me strangely, probably because he's never seen me drink Captain Morgan before. I've been trying to stay away from it after I drank too much in Vegas and then clocked my ex across the side of his head with my purse. Of course, it was just after I caught him and my best friend wrapped together like wrestlers in a strangle hold. But nonetheless, Captain Morgan makes me squirrelly, to say the least. But tonight, it's going to be Captain, because I'm going home alone anyway.

While the band stops playing to take a break, we chat about our kids.

"So, how are your daughters doing these days?" I ask.

"Oh, they're good," he says. "I've got another grandbaby due any day now," as he grabs for his wallet on the bar. "My oldest is 3 already," he says, pulling out a picture for me.

"Oh, she is adorable," I tell him. "She looks like her mom."

It's true. She's got big blue eyes and blond hair, but that smile is just like her mama. He's beaming with pride as he takes the picture and tucks it back in his wallet.

"I can't wait to be a grandma," I tell him. "I mean, I can wait, but I'm looking forward to it."

"Yeah, it's pretty fun watching your children become parents," he says.

"At first, I thought maybe I would have more kids, give it another try if I met someone who hadn't had kids, someone who wanted one of their own, or ours," I tell him. "But now I feel like I'm over that. My kids are older and I need to focus on them right now, with everything they're going through."

"That makes sense," he reassures me. "You should enjoy your time with them, enjoy the ages that they are."

"I wanted more kids, actually," I tell him. "But my ex wanted to be done, so he went and took care of that about six weeks after our daughter was born."

"Well, it's probably meant to be, then," he says.

The band starts playing Van Morrison's 'Brown Eyed Girl' and I'm glad because I don't really want to think about it anymore. I feel like if it's meant to be, it will happen. And I feel like I'm done having kids anyway, except for maybe John. He's the only exception. My friend makes another attempt at convincing me to dance.

"Alright," he says. "What about now?"

"Oh, alright," I say, knowing full well that I won't stop at one dance once I get started.

When we get on the dance floor, I'm not really sure what to expect. I wonder if he'll grab my hand and twirl me around, or maybe pull me close. At first, we dance alone, doing our own thing. Me, grinding my ass trying to look like Shakira, snapping my fingers with my hands at my sides and clapping every once in a while, and him, turning in circles and tapping his foot, arms in the air, hands coming together in unison with me to the beat of the music. Then, he grabs my hand and pulls me closer, my left hand holding around his back, and my right held inside his. He turns me, not too fast so my head is spinning, but just right, just like it should be, at least for me. It reminds me of John again, and a little bit of life. Like we need to do our own thing for a little while, but someday come back together to dance. Maybe a slow song, holding me closer, then something fast where we're twisting and turning in circles. We dance a couple of songs together before the leader of the band announces it is midnight. We head to the bar to grab our drinks, then head back to the dance floor as the countdown begins.

"3, 2, 1…" the crowd says in unison. "Happy New Year!"

We're standing on the dance floor, and he leans in for a kiss. I'm hesitant because I don't want him to get the wrong idea, don't want him to think there is something more to this. I lean toward him and our lips meet just briefly. It's my first kiss as a single woman on New Year's Eve. I know that it's just a kiss, just a dog smooch, a bird peck, really. And yet, it's not just a kiss for me. For all the kisses I have had in my life, I will remember this one forever.

He pulls away from me, and suddenly I feel like I should go home.

"Well, I'm going to get going," I tell him, heading back to our chairs at the bar.

"Don't you want to stay?" he asks.

"No, my kids are coming in the morning and I want to get a good night's sleep tonight," I tell him.

"C'mon," he says. "Stay for one more drink."

"I had a great time tonight," I say, smiling, avoiding his pleading altogether. "Thanks for dancing with me."

He winks as I turn back at him, then head out the door. My heart is warm as I face the cold, misty, first of January night alone.

Driving across town, an old 80s song comes on the radio, Dan Fogelberg's 'Auld Lang Syne.'

We drank a toast to innocence

We drank a toast to time

Reliving in our eloquence

Another 'Auld Lang Syne'

It reminds me of an old high school friend of mine who was a music fan like me. He would invite me over to his house once in awhile and we would sit and listen to music in his bedroom. The boom box would shake on high volume with songs from Fogelberg and James Taylor. He played it over and over again for me, just because I liked it so much. In fact, the first time I heard it, I was with him. It was December then, and I was still trying to get over my first real boyfriend, a college boy who had broken up with me that summer. The song is a perfect end to the night, a ballad about old friends and lost loves that are better as a memory, and it ends just as I pull in the driveway.

When I get in the house, it feels cold, damp, and lonely. It always seems that way when my kids are gone. I check the temperature on the thermostat. It's 68 degrees but feels more like 50. I miss my kids so badly. I text my oldest son. It is almost 12:30 but I just know that he will still be up.

Happy New Year babe!

Happy New Year mom

How did you celebrate?

We're at a hotel, watching the ball drop on TV

Well that's fun

Everybody is sleeping but me

Who's everybody?

Bennett and Becca, and the girls

Where's your dad?

Somewhere with Janet, they're going to be back soon

What did you do all night?

We went swimming for a while, then had pizza, then they went to the bar

Well, I'm sorry you're alone

It's ok, we had fun

I'll see you in the morning, ok?

We're going to grandma and grandpa's house to hang out and play cards and games

OK, sounds good

I love you

Love you too mom

I want to take my phone and hurl it across the room. It reminds me of another night I felt the same, the night my phone actually did fly out of my hand, the night my ex told me he had feelings for some homewrecker that he ended up fucking in the front seat of her car a few miles from our house. And now he's probably off "making love to" my old best friend in the stairwell of the hotel while my 13-year-old sits alone babysitting her kids. I have the best of intentions to keep calm, but I pick it up and chuck it at the mirror directly across from my bed, shattering the mirror into hundreds of tiny little pieces.

"Oh my fucking God," I say to my cold bedroom walls. "I cannot believe this is my life."

I don't know what makes me more angry: the idea of my son being by himself, the reality that my ex is truly fucking my old best friend, or that for the first time since I was 17-years-old, I am alone on New Year's Eve. I grab for my laptop. I just want to listen to some music so I open up Jango.

With tears streaming down my face, I login to Facebook to update my status.

Pray to God my life turns out better than this.

And that's just all there is to say right now. Besides Happy Fucking New Year.

For days, I think about John, about what's happened in the past few weeks, the drinking, the horrible hangovers, the bad choices I've made. Maybe these things are just me, maybe John, maybe some of his friends. Maybe it's a little bit of everything.

I want to know what really happened that night after I left the bar. I was so wasted that I basically blacked out, remembering nothing after I left. I feel like John had to have been the one who was in my house. Someone was. Maybe I just want it to be him. And if it wasn't him, I have no idea who it was. In the morning before the kids come home, I send a text to John.

So I hope I enjoyed the other night

I think you should delete my number and get a life

I think you're the one who should get a life actually

Just as I text it, I regret it. But why in the hell would John tell me to get a life? He knows that I've got one, and it's a messy one, to say the least. What an asshole.

A few days later, I log into Facebook, and I see John's name pop up in chat. I want to apologize, but I feel like it started with him telling me to get a life. I want to start over, like I've never met him at all. The only thing I can think to do is just completely disconnect from him, like that's the best thing right now. I skip over to my Facebook profile, find John's profile and unfriend him. Then, I delete his number on my phone and work on getting a life.

I can see it now, even as I craft this story, that his text was his way of saying goodbye without having to, because I didn't want to, because I couldn't do it myself. All I wanted was for him to give me some time, time to grow up, time to be alone with my kids, make a new kind of normal for us, shape myself into a woman without a man, and recover from all of the hurts and betrayal that I lived with for so many years. All I feel is toxic. Whatever the reasons, we weren't meant to be then. It was exactly what I needed when I needed it the most. I didn't see it then, but I do now. Maybe someone like John will come back around. And maybe someday, it will be the love story I always wanted.

www.ingramcontent.com/pod-product-compliance
Lightning Source LLC
Chambersburg PA
CBHW060803120626
46557CB00001B/65